Bamberger's

NEW JERSEY'S GREATEST STORE

M ICHAEL J. L ISICKY

THE
History
PRESS

Published by The History Press
Charleston, SC
www.historypress.net

First published 2016

Manufactured in the United States

ISBN 978.1.46713.644.0

Library of Congress Control Number: 2016942429

If you're interested in department store history, buy his books.
—*Philadelphia Inquirer*

Retail fans can now take a stroll down memory lane with Lisicky, a department store historian.
—*Boston Globe*

Lisicky is probably the only department store historian I know. He's an oboist with the Baltimore Symphony but his true passion is those great brick-and-mortar stores that were so much a part of our lives.
—*Tampa Tribune*

Like veterans of a noble cause—a battle or an expedition—former employees of Woodward & Lothrop came forward to share their memories after the recent column on Lisicky's book. Customers did, too.
—*Washington Post*

You might think of Michael Lisicky's obsession with department stores as an orchestral tone poem for a single oboe: at turns plaintive and raucous, eloquent and funny, with unpredictable little swerves.
—*Baltimore Sun*

From the late 1960s until the early 1980s, Bamberger's used an illustration of the once-busy Newark main floor in its employee handbook. *Courtesy of Paul Coghlan.*

To every former department store employee and customer who remains proud and loyal to this very day, long after the store's doors have closed.

Contents

Acknowledgements

A ny type of historical book could never be possible without the assistance and archival resources of libraries, historical societies and museums. I want to thank Thomas Ankner and the Newark Public Library, the staff at the New Jersey Historical Society, librarian/archivist William Peniston and the Newark Museum, Bill Leaver and the Fritz Behnke History Museum, the Jewish Federation of Greater Metrowest New Jersey, the Metuchen-Edison Historical Society and Nancy Piwowar and the Historical Society of Plainfield. The newspaper archives of the *Newark Evening News*, the *Newark Star-Ledger*, the *New York Times*, the *Jersey Journal* and the *Trenton Times* proved invaluable to this project. The Mergent Archives database of corporate annual reports has also proved to be an essential and invaluable resource.

Archival documents must be supplemented by personal memories, and former buyer Ken Allan and former Newark mayor Kenneth A. Gibson were so generous with their recollections. Sincere appreciation goes to Senator Cory Booker, along with the assistance of Newark office press secretary Thomas Pietrykoski, for his contribution that perfectly defined Bamberger's important cultural and commercial role in Newark and throughout the Garden State. Former Bamberger's executives interviewed throughout the book helped give the insider's view of this amazingly successful business. Raymond Harris helped remember and document even the simplest dish served at the store's restaurants. Locating his whereabouts would not have been possible without Larry Davis's help. Regional department stores, and their traditions, may have largely disappeared. You can't see them or touch them, but their surviving recipes and preparations can maybe help you taste or smell them. I find recipes to be essential to these types of books, and I thank former restaurant manager Raymond Harris for his memory. The main downtown restaurant closed in 1955, but the steamed hot dogs and orange drink served at the snack bars throughout the stores still evoke happy thoughts. Too bad the brand name remains unknown. A special thank-you also goes out to Betty Detmer for her culinary assistance. And as always, this series of department store history and memory books could not continue without the motivation of Jan Whitaker and David Sullivan. I am also grateful for the generous support from the Howard and Tillie Needleman Charitable Trust.

And here's to my wife, Sandy. Ten books and maybe counting? Who knows. She helps make these projects readable. Poor thing.

Iconic businesses like Bamberger's, Kresge's and Hahne's helped shape downtown Newark and indeed the whole city during the early part of the twentieth century. Not only did Bamberger's help spur economic growth in Newark and create jobs, but it helped build memories for families that lasted a lifetime and heralded Newark as a center for New Jersey culture and commerce. The history of Bamberger's is an indelible part of the history of New Jersey, and it remains as a great testimony to our city's and state's profoundly impactful entrepreneurial spirit.

Senator Cory Booker (D-NJ)
Mayor of Newark (2006–13)

Introduction

When I grew up in New Jersey, the state had only two area codes: 201 and 609; 201 meant North Jersey, and 609 meant South Jersey. Residents of the Garden State were very protective of their image and proudly defended their state to visitors and late-night talk show hosts. The entire state bonded together whenever the state's reputation was attacked, but behind the scenes, New Jersey was divided between its northern half and southern half, at least in my eyes. "201" meant the Mets and the Empire State Building, while "609" stood for the Phillies and William Penn. "201" was the Meadowlands, and "609" was the Pine Barrens. "201" had subs and heroes, and "609" sold hoagies. "201" had Newark, and "609" had Camden. The list can go on forever. Down south, we never called it "Jersey" or asked, "What exit?" For us, New Jersey ultimately was one flawed and somewhat divided state, but it was everybody's home.

I was born in Camden and raised in Cherry Hill. By the 1950s, my community had started covering its plentiful farmlands with homes filled with families who had escaped city living. It was the utopian suburbs, the perfect American dream. Up until the early 1960s, it was known as Delaware Township. But when Delaware Township wanted its own post office, the application was denied. There was already a Delaware Township, but it was located in North Jersey's Hunterdon County. Delaware Township needed a new name, and the decision seemed relatively easy. We already had the Cherry Hill Inn, the Cherry Hill Farm and the brand-new Cherry Hill Mall. On November 7, 1961, Delaware Township voters officially approved a new name: Cherry Hill.

The Cherry Hill Mall was the community's most visible and active landmark. Planned over years and built in sections, the enclosed mall was spearheaded by Philadelphia's Strawbridge & Clothier department store. But when the shopping center embarked on its second phase, Strawbridge & Clothier elected not to compete with any other Philadelphia-area department store. Instead, Strawbridge's approved Newark-based Bamberger's as the mall's second anchor store. Bamberger's was little known to "609" residents but was regarded in the industry as a sturdy and reliable retailer. Its association with the powerful and famous R.H. Macy & Co. also gave it validity. Bamberger's entry into Cherry Hill was meant to complement Strawbridge & Clothier and the mall's smaller shops. It wasn't intended to dominate Strawbridge's, but by the 1970s, Bamberger's Cherry Hill had blossomed into the top-grossing suburban department store in the Philadelphia/South Jersey area.

As a kid who was fascinated by department store logos and names, I was intrigued by the Bamberger's name. Did the area really need a Bamberger's store? We had John Wanamaker, Strawbridge & Clothier, Gimbels and Lits. But for some reason, we also had one Bamberger's. You had to do your research and be interested enough to learn that Bamberger's had its roots in Newark, along with its mysterious flagship presence. Newark certainly didn't have the reputation of being a shopping and social mecca. But I was intrigued, and I became further intrigued in the early 1980s when the Bamberger's advertisements stopped listing Newark as the first name in their directory of locations. Advertisements listed "star-studded" North Jersey names, and by the time I graduated from high school in 1982, the Newark store was usually the last in line, with limited selections and hours. My interest in Bamberger's grew.

This interest warranted my first real shopping trip to Newark in 1982. My brother and I found Bamberger's to be a big old store with a nice amount of activity and a big city feel, along with an unexpected offering of food products. Growing up in New Jersey, it was easy to look the other way and forgive images of blight and failed urban redevelopment. You learned to turn your head while driving by refineries and eternally brown marshlands along the Turnpike. So we weren't alarmed by Bamberger's bricked-over display windows along Market Street. Bamberger's in Newark was a big surprise for the two of us. It was alive, and so was its competitor Hahne's, seemingly made entirely of wood. It wasn't our only time in downtown Newark, and we returned whenever we could. We certainly didn't have these types of businesses in Camden, our local city.

Into the early 1980s, an illustration of the exterior of the Newark store appeared on the employee handbook cover. The image showed some of the ornate detail on the store's Market Street storefront. *Courtesy of Paul Coughlan.*

Just as New Jersey is divided into two different sections, Bamberger's story is also divided. Louis Bamberger and his partners built an amazing emporium in a growing yet troubled industrial city. By the 1960s, Bamberger's knew its future was in New Jersey's suburbs, not in Newark.

So the company's story goes back and forth between its explosive growth in powerful shopping malls and challenges at its antiquated and obsolete downtown Newark store. Just as one aspect of the business succeeded and blossomed, the other part struggled and downsized. It's the city versus the suburbs, a conflict played out in metropolitan areas across the country. The great American clash between downtown decline and suburban ascent seemed magnified in Newark and North Jersey.

Bamberger's "darling" status of the Macy organization was largely due to its educated and risk-taking leadership. Some of the department store industry's most talented executives made their way through the Newark headquarters and eventually brought their talent to other Macy divisions. Many former employees of defunct department stores remain in contact and occasionally gather and reminisce, but former Bamberger employees are intensely loyal to their former workplace, seemingly much more so than other former department store employees. Maybe it's their fierce pride in the Garden State.

There is one last thing to say about this store. As a former South Jersey resident and shopper, we never called it "Bam's." Nobody I knew called it "Bam's." It was Bamberger's. But when I delved into company information, newspaper archives and Internet groups, I often saw the word "Bam's." I'm not the kind of person who likes nicknames, but as I've grown older, I accept them more as endearments. "Bam's" doesn't roll off my tongue, and it probably never will. Regardless of the name preference, "Bam's" or Bamberger's will always be remembered as New Jersey's Greatest Store.

One of America's Great Merchants

The name of Louis Bamberger is associated with the finest tradition of merchandising, Jewish communal life, and cultural advancement.
—Jewish Chronicle, *June 20, 1941*

Before he arrived in Newark and became one of the city's greatest merchants and philanthropists, Louis Bamberger learned his trade and honed his skills in Baltimore. Bamberger was born on May 15, 1855, to Elkan and Theresa Hutzler Bamberger. Elkan operated a small "dry goods and fancy business" alongside his brothers David and Moses. Named Bamberger Brothers, it was located in the center of Baltimore's retail and wholesale district at 71 North Howard Street. In February 1853, the Bamberger Brothers business dissolved "by mutual consent" as Elkan Bamberger bought out his brothers' interest. In 1858, Louis's uncle, Moses Hutzler, established his own dry goods business, which grew into one of Baltimore's iconic department stores. In 1869, at age fourteen, Louis Bamberger joined the Hutzler Brothers firm as a stock boy. At a weekly salary of four dollars, Bamberger swept Hutzler's floors and ran errands, but he soon worked his way up the company ranks.[1] After learning further skills from his uncle and cousins, Louis rejoined his father's dry goods business alongside his brother Julius and nephew Edgar. In 1887, Louis and his father, Elkan, sold his company to Hutzler Brothers, and the two men left for New York. Julius and Edgar remained in Baltimore with the Hutzler store, and Louis and Elkan opened a wholesale operation in New York.[2] While in New York, Louis

Louis Bamberger poses with employees in February 1893, shortly after the store's grand opening earlier in the month. L. Bamberger & Co.'s first venture was located at Market Street and Library Court, in the former Hill & Craig building. *Courtesy of the Newark Public Library.*

also worked as a buyer for "several Western department stores."[3] However, Louis ultimately wanted to operate his own retail operation. In 1892, Louis learned that a Newark store, Hill & Craig, located at Market Street at Library Court, had filed for bankruptcy and liquidation. Bamberger quickly purchased Hill & Craig's assets and hoped to establish his own retail firm in the booming industrial city. Newark was a "thriving center of both industry and agriculture" that was underserved by commercial firms.

Historian Charles F. Cummings stated, "Newark was one of the [top four] most important industrial cities in all of America." By 1910, 70 percent of Newarkers were immigrants and most transplanted families earned their wages as factory workers. They eagerly accepted employment but "worked hard and died young."[4] Though the industries offered abundant employment, workers received modest pay and were forced to live in substandard and crowded housing options. However, factory owners involved in the city's chemical, beer, silver and utility industries also resided in the city. These wealthier families lived along High Street and in such neighborhoods as Forest Hill. But "small efforts" by Newark's shop owners were made to court Newark's middle- to upper-class residents, who were often forced to travel to New York City and purchase necessities and luxuries. When Louis Bamberger first visited Newark and observed the Hill & Craig business, he walked throughout Newark's business district, studied the various stores and counted its crowds. A 1941 article about Louis Bamberger stated, "He wanted to make a connection with the retail end of the business and believed that Newark provided an opportunity to do this."[5]

Louis Bamberger soon learned that the purchase of Hill & Craig was more complicated than he had imagined. Bamberger examined its stock and realized that "he had bought far more [goods] than his experience as a sales agent for several New York firms would permit him to handle."[6] He enlisted the help of family and associates to sell off the excess goods to various surplus firms but was unsuccessful. Bamberger partnered with his brother-in-law Louis M. Frank and a young rubber goods salesman, Felix Fuld. The two men invested in Louis Bamberger's new company and helped Louis prepare the store for a liquidation sale. On December 13, 1892, the bankrupt Hill & Craig store reopened under new ownership and held a public sale. A sale advertisement declared, "All Goods Offered at a Great Sacrifice!" The overwhelmingly successful sale encouraged the three men to quickly add fresh stock and remain in business. Louis's aspiration to operate his own retail store was formally realized on February 1, 1893. The firm was renamed L. Bamberger & Co., with Bamberger, Fuld and Frank as equal partners.[7]

L. Bamberger & Co. embraced many of the revolutionary business practices that helped build other successful large firms in other major cities. Fixed pricing, guaranteed returns and an extensive offering of goods set L. Bamberger & Co. apart from other Newark retailers. Louis also developed close working relationships with many supply houses that provided the company with quality goods and competitive prices. Frank I. Liveright, one of Louis Bamberger's closest business associates, called Louis "the most ethical man I've ever met" and cited his employee, customer and supplier loyalty as "company hallmarks." With Louis Frank in charge of merchandise and Felix Fuld responsible for sales and advertising, Bamberger established a group of leaders that pushed the firm into expansion.

The former two-story Hill & Craig quickly proved too small for the growing concern. In 1898, the firm moved to the northeast corner of Market and Halsey Streets and doubled in size.[8] Within six short years, the

L. Bamberger & Co.'s original store opened for business on February 1, 1893, at the corner of Market and Halsey Streets. The business, according to the photograph, was called "Bamberger's Annex," and its windows promoted it as a "High Grade Store." *Courtesy of the Newark Public Library.*

company employed approximately five hundred workers and boasted total sales of over $1.3 million. Felix Fuld managed the company's workforce, and the store was known as a good employer. Fuld termed his employees "co-workers," and vacation pay, salary commissions, sick pay and death benefits were put into practice as early as 1901. The firm continually increased its customer base with exclusive merchandise offerings and special services. L. Bamberger & Co. offered home delivery on horse-drawn wagons and sleds throughout New Jersey. In later years, it was one of the first stores to switch to motor vehicle deliveries.[9] In May 1901, the store installed New Jersey's first escalator. The moving stairway that "stirred Newark" was called the "Reno Escalator" and frightened some customers and insurers.[10] As the company continued on its successful path, it sometimes overpowered the three businessmen.[11] They closely counted all sales transactions and advertising expenditures so that they remained current on all financial obligations. The store continually removed walls and expanded in order to increase sales square footage. L. Bamberger & Co. knew that the firm could not remain at its current site permanently.

On August 4, 1910, L. Bamberger & Co. received some devastating news. Louis M. Frank had died suddenly from apoplexy while vacationing in Lucerne, Switzerland, with his wife, Caroline Bamberger Frank. Upon the death of Louis Frank, L. Bamberger & Co. incorporated its business, which named Louis Bamberger president, Felix Fuld vice-president and treasurer and associate Frank I. Liveright secretary. The incorporation secured L.

THE GREATER BAMBERGER STORE
FORMAL OPENING NEXT WEDNESDAY

Five more days and the great idea, born twenty long years ago, will crystallize into shape. Five more days and the newest and possibly the finest of America's Great Stores will open its doors to an expectant public. No one will ever know the days and weeks and months of labor and worry and concentration that this great structure has cost those who are responsible for its being, nor will any one realize the earnestness and thoroughness with which even the smallest details of the great work were prosecuted. Greater Bamberger's is now a reality, and when the doors swing open next Wednesday the people of New Jersey will behold a perfect store. This is the first of a series of very remarkable opening announcements that have been prepared. Watch for these announcements and read them carefully—aside from their artistic value; they will tell you many interesting things about a very interesting new store. They will unfold the story of the great idea from its inception to its complete realization. Consult your calendar and see that next Wednesday is kept open—the inauguration of the new Bamberger Store is too important a function for you to miss. L. BAMBERGER & CO., Newark, N. J.

A series of ornate advertisements announced the opening of "Greater Bamberger's" in October 1912. This announcement promised, "The people of New Jersey will behold a perfect store." L. Bamberger & Co. assured customers that the inauguration of the store was "too important a function to miss." *Collection of the author.*

Bamberger & Co.'s future. The firm set its sights on a parcel of property just west of its current store. Located within the streets bounded by Market, Halsey, Washington and Bank, numerous small storefronts filled the city block. Bamberger was afraid to publicly announce his intentions and quietly acquired the properties through a realty company. He feared that some store owners would hold out for exorbitant fees while others would refuse to sell for any price. After it finally secured all desired properties, L. Bamberger & Co. enlisted the services of renowned Chicago architect Jarvis Hunt to design a new home for "New Jersey's Greatest Store." Once the plans for the new building were officially announced, the company stated, "The new Bamberger Store, even now, is one of the showplaces of Newark. What will it be when the doors [of the new location] are finally thrown open?"[12]

Chapter 2

The Always Busy Store

L. Bamberger & Co. opened its new 500,000-square-foot, eight-story department store on October 16, 1912, to great fanfare. The massive terra-cotta building, designed by Jarvis Hunt, became known as the "Great White Store." The company officially announced that the new store was "a monument to the minds of those who created it—a lasting tribute to the buying public that made the great work possible."[13] Former company secretary Frank Liveright recalled, "We didn't give out souvenirs at the opening, but the public took care of that itself. On opening day our restaurant was crowded; when we closed that night, almost all of the cutlery stamped 'Bamberger's' and the crockery with the Bamberger monogram were taken away as souvenirs."[14] An article in the *New York Times* cited the building's "pleasing façade" and "artistic charm." The newspaper continued, "It is pleasing to see that the owners of a big business like that of Bamberger have recognized the moral and lasting worth of a retail store, beautiful to look at."[15] With 144 feet of Market Street frontage, the structure represented a $2 million investment. This new "perfect store" contained sixteen elevators, an "air washing" device that kept the store free from "dust and other impurities," a four-hundred-seat dining hall, a six-hundred-seat concert hall and a hospital with a resident physician and nurses. Two tunnels connected the old and new Bamberger operations, and its former location transitioned into a warehouse and delivery facility. The *New York Evening Mail* newspaper stated, "This institution is a credit to the industrial progress of the State of New Jersey. If we could persuade New York stores to conduct their business

Crowds form at the corner of Market and Halsey Streets on opening day, October 16, 1912. The building on the right side of the photograph is the former Bamberger's store that operated from 1898 to 1912. Numerous delivery wagons are located alongside the former Bamberger's retail store. The former store served as a warehouse until 1930. *Courtesy of the Newark Public Library.*

on the same lines of justice and integrity, the millennium would be close at hand."[16] At the corner of Market and Halsey Streets, a large round clock jutted out from the new store, and the site became one of Newark's most popular meeting places.

Former mayor Kenneth A. Gibson credits Newark's growth to the city's water supply. "The reason Newark became such an industrial base was due to the quality of its water. It gave the dye for chemicals better quality and helped develop many of Newark's huge breweries, such as Ballantine's and Krueger's. The water out of the faucet was of such high quality that people came to work with empty bottles," says Gibson. The new Bamberger store portrayed itself as a symbol of Newark's industrial success. It celebrated and catered to the different demographics of the growing city. As the building neared completion, the company stated, "The new Bamberger store is not a store for the classes, nor yet is it a store for the masses. It is a store for both masses and classes—it is a store for all the people!…Newark is a monument to all the people—rich and poor. It is a tribute to the industry, thrift and loyalty of the great buying public. It is the people's store."[17]

With its expanded size, the Great White Store increased its offerings and brought forth a new era of innovative products and services. One of the company's most valuable leaders was Walter Moler. Moler became

The first section of the modern L. Bamberger & Co. flagship store opened in 1912. The Bamberger store helped celebrate Newark's 250th anniversary in 1916 with a large wreath placed over the Market Street doors. *Courtesy of the Newark Public Library.*

the head of public relations and brought notoriety to the company with unique events that captured local and national attention. He helped inaugurate an exposition of Newark-made products. The exhibit proved so successful that it was repeated in 1914 with President Woodrow Wilson at the official exhibit opening.[18] Throughout the teens, Moler also presented fashion shows, war bond drives, Christmas celebrations and celebrity visits to the department store. Arguably his most visible promotions were deliveries by the company's airplane. In May 1919, Bamberger's purchased a Curtiss JN-4D training plane and planned to make express deliveries by plane to suburban communities and locations along the New Jersey shore. On August 16, 1919, the department store completed its "first heart-of-the-city delivery" when a bag of silverware from Bridgeport, Connecticut, was dropped by parachute near the Memorial Building. Just three days later, aviator Edwin F. Ballough landed a small plane on the roof of the Newark store after circling the building numerous times. Ballough dropped off a New York City passenger for a day of shopping. Seven years later, Bamberger's conducted the nation's first

On September 13, 1916, Bamberger's opened its popular basement store. The basement was viewed as a "store within a store" and became an important component to the Bamberger's business, especially under R.H. Macy's 1929 acquisition. The store basement grew to four underground levels with two floors devoted to selling space. *Collection of the author.*

overseas business transaction with an airplane delivery of French perfume. The department store also extended its fascination of air transport to its younger customers and established the Bamberger Aero Club in 1925. Young men participated in future aviation discussions along with model airplane demonstrations and competitions throughout the 1930s and 1940s.

By 1920, L. Bamberger & Co. had declared its operation "One of America's Great Stores." It proudly put its business up against any of

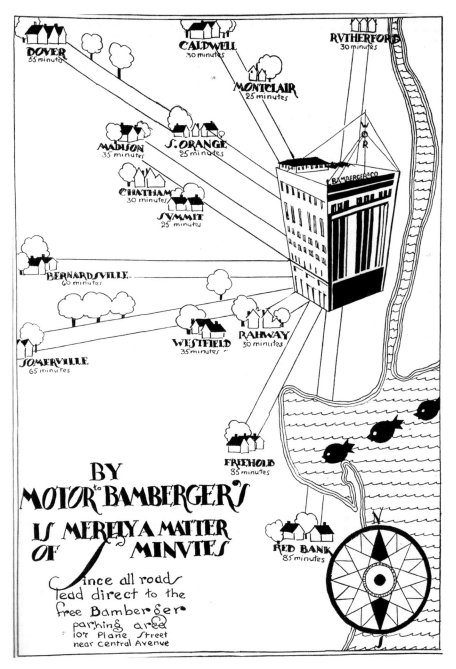

By the 1920s, many middle- and upper-class Newarkers had relocated to North Jersey's suburban communities. Bamberger's frequently acknowledged easy automobile access to its Newark store. The department store also promoted abundant downtown parking options for suburban customers. *Courtesy of the Newark Public Library.*

the country's other leading stores. Since Newark was smaller than other urban commercial centers such as New York City, Philadelphia, Chicago and Boston, L. Bamberger & Co. promoted its extensive selection of merchandise alongside specialized and personal customer service. "You have come in contact with scores of stores in your travels. You have purchased in many. You have had an opportunity to compare the service of all. But if you have ever shopped in Bamberger's you will instantly note a different kind of atmosphere pervading the house. People seem kinder, more able, more willing, more eager. Bamberger's is not a store that has won country-wide prominence because of one thing. No! But through the happy combination of many unusual features, this store naturally assumes the leadership."[19]

The bond between Louis Bamberger and Felix Fuld further strengthened in 1918 when Fuld married Bamberger's sister and widow of former partner Louis Frank. His marriage to the former Caroline Bamberger Frank brought Fuld directly into the Bamberger family.

Much of the success of L. Bamberger & Co. was due to its management team. Store executives, including secretary Frank Liveright, Louis's nephew Edgar S. Bamberger and publicity director Walter Moler, gathered for daily morning meetings. Moler, with support and encouragement from Edgar Bamberger, proposed an in-store radio station. They claimed that a radio station combined innovation with promotion and could provide invaluable attention to the department store. In addition, the broadcasts were designed to promote the sale of "new-fangled" radio receiver sets sold at the large store.[20] On February 22, 1922, WOR radio went on the air with a 250-watt reconditioned transmitter. Broadcast from a corner in the store's furniture and sporting goods department, WOR debuted with a recording of Al Jolson singing "April Showers." Jolson's voice was broadcast as a lone microphone was dragged alongside the phonograph. Bamberger initially requested the call letters "WLB," but they were already assigned to a Minneapolis station. Over the next several months, WOR's signal was strengthened and its programs were received in Brooklyn, Staten Island and Asbury Park.[21] Within a year, WOR's improved signal was picked up in London. WOR gained notoriety in October 1922 when Sir Thomas Lipton became the first person to broadcast his voice across the Atlantic Ocean. During the historic event, Lipton spoke into a microphone at London's Selfridge's department store, and his voice was received inside the Newark department store. Bamberger's WOR radio station featured appearances by luminaries such as Charlie Chaplin and Thomas Edison, along with local personalities such as Jersey City's Andy Gregory, the "Banjo Wizard."

For five years, Bamberger's Newark store housed the WOR station, until it was relocated to Kearney.

On October 30, 1922, six hundred dignitaries, from politicians to various executives from many East Coast department stores, gathered at Bamberger's and celebrated its new annex building at Market and Washington Streets. Located directly next to the 1912 store, the annex increased the store's square footage by almost 120,000 square feet. Jarvis Hunt, the architect of the 1912 structure, also designed the annex and created a unified front along Market and Washington Streets. The addition allowed for an "airy, well-ventilated basement" that housed 146 selling departments. "For years, we have realized the need in Newark for a store within a store—where full regular lines of low-priced, but reliable merchandise would be found and where the usual type of Bamberger service would prevail," stated a company advertisement. "Bamberger's Basement will handle only dependable merchandise. The prices will be low, but not at the sacrifice of quality." By 1922, L. Bamberger & Co.'s workforce had swelled to more than three thousand co-workers.

Bamberger's offered a customer parking service that transported customers from a private lot to the store entrance on Washington Street. The image shows the once-ornate display windows and decorative exterior lighting. *Courtesy of the Newark Public Library.*

In addition to being a savvy merchant, Louis Bamberger was one of the community's greatest benefactors. One of Bamberger's most visible philanthropic actions was an initial $500,000 donation to the Newark Museum. The museum was founded in 1909 by director John Cotton Dana and featured everything from one of the world's greatest modern art collections to everyday items of worth and beauty. Over several years, Dana and Bamberger developed a close personal relationship, and both men respected each other's institutions. "Dana felt that a department store was a better museum than some museums," states Newark Museum librarian and archivist William A. Peniston. "Bamberger and Dana saw eye to eye and had a real rapport." Like Bamberger, Dana wanted the Newark Museum to be open to all classes. "Dana had a real grudge against museums that were located away from the city and the people. He saw [those museums] as elitist." On January 19, 1923, Bamberger provided his initial gift for "a completed building suitable for its purpose."[22] Bamberger continued, "I have felt for a long time that inasmuch as I had made a success of my business in Newark, I owed the city something.…Newark has needed a museum building and I am glad that it is possible for me to help the city have one." Bamberger enlisted the help of his store's architect, Jarvis Hunt, and personally supervised the museum's construction. He became president of the museum's board of directors and continually increased his financial contributions to well over $1 million. Louis Bamberger's civic commitment did not end at the Newark Museum. He contributed to the Newark Community Chest, the United Jewish Appeal campaign, the YMHA, Newark's Beth Israel Hospital, the Hebrew Benevolent and Orphan Asylum Society and the New Jersey Historical Society. Bamberger even included a small branch of the Newark Museum in his downtown Newark store. Felix Fuld and his wife, Caroline Bamberger Fuld, followed Louis in many of his philanthropic efforts. Felix Fuld was regarded as one of the city's greatest organizers of charitable campaigns that supported many Newark-area institutions.

Bamberger's was innovative when it came to print promotions that benefited co-workers and customers. L. Bamberger & Co.'s *Counter Currents* publication was introduced in October 1913, predating the many in-house publications created by national department stores by the 1920s. *Counter Currents* recognized store programs and services, as well as employee accomplishments and announcements.

In the 1920s, a number of affluent Newark residents began to relocate to North Jersey's growing suburban communities. As automobile travel

CHARM

One of Bamberger's earliest promotions was *Charm* magazine. The fashion magazine featured articles and items of interest for middle- to upper-class New Jerseyites. The innovative publication was produced from 1924 to 1932. Subtitled "The Magazine of New Jersey Home Interests," this cover was of the June 1930 issue. *Collection of the author.*

became more popular and prevalent, Bamberger's wanted to hold onto its higher-income customer. The Holland Tunnel, built in 1927, allowed easy access to Manhattan for automobile travelers, and Bamberger's hoped to prevent customers from bypassing Newark for the New York City stores. Under the direction of public relations head Walter Moler, *Charm* magazine was launched in February 1924. The monthly publication was designed to inform customers of fashion trends, relate human-interest stories and appeal directly to higher-income New Jerseyans. The company presented *Charm* as "the most effective way to reach the well-off northern New Jersey market— what the editors termed the mass of class, the group of people whose incomes are sufficient to gratify their desires."[23] *Charm* was geared toward the "better educated customer," but as was the practice of other large American department stores, it encouraged those with moderate incomes to trade higher with purchases. The publication *Bamberger's Department Store, Charm Magazine, and the Culture of Consumption in New Jersey, 1924–1932* states:

> Charm*'s largest audience, then, was not its most elite class of readers, but Bamberger's far more numerous middle-class customers, those who may have been somewhat well-off but were certainly not so rich or well connected.* Charm *encouraged them to conjure up a personal identification with the social elite and to associate that identity with the Newark store.*

Throughout the latter half of the 1920s, *Charm* magazine was extremely successful and kept the Bamberger name "before the public in the most favorable light."[24]

Despite the demographic changes and increased retail competition within the city of Newark, L. Bamberger & Co. expanded its already massive operation. When Newark City Council updated its zoning ordinance and permitted buildings as high as 200 feet, Louis Bamberger announced a fourteen-story addition along Washington Street in June 1925. In November 1926, Bamberger increased the building's height to sixteen stories. At a cost of over $14 million, it was Bamberger's most expensive project to date. However, its construction along the Bank Street side proved complicated and moved slowly as cracks developed in the walls of the adjacent Prudential Insurance building.[25] Completed in 1929, the new addition doubled the size of the department store to a total area of 1.2 million square feet. This

Above: The fully completed L. Bamberger & Co. downtown Newark flagship store stands proudly at Market and Washington Streets. *Courtesy of the Newark Public Library.*

Opposite: In August 1925, L. Bamberger & Co. acknowledged the thousands of New Jersey residents and visitors who shopped at "One of America's Great Stores." This advertisement listed the many special services offered at the Newark institution, from golf instruction to musical instrument and fountain pen repair, and thanked customers who came to see the home of WOR radio and *Charm* magazine. The WOR radio antennas are shown on the store's roof. *Collection of the author.*

Some of the Services of L. Bamberger & Co.

IN YOUR OWN HOME ~

WOR Radio Broadcasting Station
"Charm," the Bamberger Magazine of New Jersey Home Interests
Interior Decorating
Piano Tuning and Repair
Phonograph Repair
WOR Radio Doctor
Sewing Machine Repair
Prompt, Efficient Mail and Telephone Order Service
Eight Toll Free Telephone Trunk Lines, including a special Shore service through our Asbury Park Service Station
The Best Delivery Service in the United States
Prepaid Shipment of Purchases Anywhere in the United States

Some of the Services of L. Bamberger & Co.

IN THE STORE ITSELF ~

Films Developed, Printed and Enlarged
Tea Room and Restaurant
Concert Ticket Office
Ask Mr. Foster Travel Information Service
Fishing and Hunting Booklets and Licenses
Golf Instruction
Golf Clubs Cleaned and Repaired
Tennis Rackets Restrung
Camera Repair
Sewing Service Shop
Cutting and Fitting Service
Consulting Dressmaker
Hemstitching, Pleating, Button Covering and Picoting
Branch Post Office
Telegrams Sent
Public Telephones
Hair Dressing and Manicuring
Children's Hair Cutting
Instructions in Lamp Shade Making and Painting, Knitting, Art Needlework and Plasticart
Making of Ribbon Bows and Novelties
Engraving of Stationery, Silverware and Toilet Articles
Monogramming of Handkerchiefs
Custom Service for Hand Embroidering
Baby Scale and Consulting Nurse
Millinery Trimming
Cutlery Repair
Mending and Dyeing of Gotham Hose
Umbrella Recovering and Repair
Jewelry Repair
Custom Jewelry Making
Beaded Bag Repair
Glove Cleaning and Repair
Curtain and Drapery Cleaning
Oriental Rug Mending
Furniture Upholstery
Renovating of Hair and Felt Mattresses
Repairing and Renovating of Box Springs
Relacquering of Brass Beds
Musical Instrument Repair
Fur Storage, Repair, Remodeling and Custom Work
Fountain Pen Repair

An Appreciation ~

To the hundreds of new patrons who have come to us this summer ~ New Yorkers summering in New Jersey, resident New Jersey men and women, transient guests from all over the United States ~ one and all of whom have expressed, in comment and in patronage, their keen satisfaction in having so great a store as L. Bamberger & Co. in their summer midst.

AUGUST 16th—and midsummer is at its height. Along the Jersey coast every hotel is filled to capacity, every cottage is crowded in hospitality. In the Jersey mountains, and in those lower elevations that still afford abundant coolness as compared with town, summer homes are all thrown wide. Everywhere there is the spirit of vacationing, with quests of rest and recreation, of new places, new faces, new friends. From all over the United States these guests have come. And because L. Bamberger & Co. has been privileged to meet so many of them —so many more than in any previous summer—we are taking this occasion to express our earnest appreciation.

HUNDREDS of persons, residents of other States, have visited L. Bamberger & Co. this summer. Many have been frank to say that they have come out of eager curiosity to inspect the store whose name has been carried into every State in the Union. Others have told us they have come to see the home of WOR and of "Charm." Many, too, have been merchants from other cities, interested in studying this store that is known as a geographical paradox—this store that in a city of less than half a million inhabitants and within the very shadow of New York City, has nevertheless achieved the stature of a great metropolitan institution.

Many New Yorkers, summering in New Jersey, have motored into Newark, some of them for the first time, and have been keenly surprised at what they have found—good motor roads, a gratuitous parking space provided by L. Bamberger & Co. and a store that in every detail compares most favorably with their favorite store or specialty shop in Manhattan.

And hundreds of New Jersey residents, already familiar with L. Bamberger & Co. by name, have this summer come to know it in much more than name—have come to know it instead as a metropolitan institution.

One and all, these thousands of new friends that L. Bamberger & Co. has made this

summer, have agreed that this store fully justifies its fame as "One of America's Great Stores."

WHY? Because in L. Bamberger & Co. these newcomers have found a store prepared to serve them in every way that a great store can. In itself Bamberger's is a most inviting place in which to shop. Large spacious aisles, roomy elevators and plenty of them. Perfect ventilation. A clientele with which even the most fastidious shopper is proud to associate. Salesmen and women of trained capacity, eager, alert, and informed, everyone an exemplar of the famous Bamberger spirit of service. And stocks of merchandise as large, as rich, as varied as those of any other good store, anywhere in America. Furthermore, these newcomers have found that here they spare themselves the tediousness of "shopping around." Everything is under one roof. And what an amazing number of things there are here under one roof! So many in fact that almost anywhere else, even in New York City, one would be obliged to go to a great many different shops and stores to find them all. Again, these newcomers have learned that Bamberger's policy of never being undersold guarantees them against ever paying more for merchandise than in any other good store. And they have quickly learned too that the slogan of "absolute satisfaction or your money back" is liberally interpreted at all times.

SO THAT, located in the summer colony of New Jersey, easily and quickly accessible from every point, a store of metropolitan standards, of metropolitan stocks, and of metropolitan service—is it any wonder that L. Bamberger & Co. has this summer, as in every summer past, made so many new friends?

We are proud of this achievement but we are still far from content. We are still eager to find new ways to serve. And nothing that lies within our power shall remain undone to widen constantly the field of our activities and to extend their range.

L. BAMBERGER & CO.

"One of America's Great Stores"

Newark, N. J.

Copyrighted, 1925, by L. Bamberger & Co.

A Few of the Many Features of the Formal Opening

October 28 to November 2, inclusive.

STREET FLOOR: The WOR Salon Orchestra will render selections during the evening.*

SECOND FLOOR: Correct Use of Linens in the Home. Exhibition of Fabric Fashions.

THIRD FLOOR: Junior League Fashion Show.* Romance of Modern Fashions.**

FOURTH FLOOR: History of the Corset, 1534-1929. Rug-making and Hand-made Boudoir Accessories.

FIFTH FLOOR: Fashions in Furniture Periods, illustrating the precision of modern reproduction.

SIXTH FLOOR: Exhibit of Contemporary Art. Rug Exhibit. Correct Use of Artificial Light.

SEVENTH FLOOR: Exhibit of Rare Birds in the Pet Shop. "Dressing Your Dinner," a playlet, at 9 p. m. Monday, and 3:30 p. m. daily from Tuesday to Saturday.

EIGHTH FLOOR: Opening of Bunnyland. Ping Pong Tournament.* Golf Celebrities.* Radio Show.*

*Monday Evening Only.
**Tuesday to Friday, inclusive.

L. BAMBERGER & CO.
"One of America's Great Stores" NEWARK, N.J.

L. BAMBERGER & CO.
NEWARK, N.J.

October 24
1929

Dear Friends:

This is a cordial invitation to attend the formal opening of the Greater Bamberger Store, from eight to ten, Monday evening, October twenty-eight.

It is to be a formal opening of an informal store...a store built on the theory that friendly and personal service has a definite place in our relations with patrons. No merchandise will be on sale that evening.

Each floor will be the scene of interesting activities during the opening evening and the entire week.

Won't you set aside Monday evening to examine with your friends each separate floor and individual shop....the result of years of planning by artists, designers, and architects of world renown....to make your shopping pleasanter and more convenient.

Cordially yours,

L. Bamberger

Left: A pamphlet announced the numerous special events held at L. Bamberger & Co.'s official October 1929 grand opening in Newark. Events during the celebration month included a performance of the store's WOR Salon Orchestra, an exhibit of rare birds and a ping-pong tournament. *Courtesy of the New Jersey Historical Society.*

Right: Though he had just sold the business one month earlier to the R.H. Macy organization, store founder Louis Bamberger served as an honorary chairman of the board until 1939 and personally invited some of the store's most loyal customers to a private tour of the expanded store on October 28, 1929. *Courtesy of the New Jersey Historical Society.*

addition made Bamberger's Newark store larger than other prominent American emporiums such as Gimbels in New York and Strawbridge & Clothier in Philadelphia.

By 1928, annual sales at Bamberger's exceeded $35 million—the fourth highest sales volume in the country. The large store touted its workforce and the "Bamberger Spirit." "Throughout the entire Bamberger store there is an atmosphere of spaciousness and of quiet earnestness of purpose," stated a company brochure.

> *Aisles are wide and uncrowded. Ceilings are high. Elevators are plentiful. Ventilation is perfect. Counter displays are bright and interesting. Merchandise is, without exception, of worthy character—the kind you can*

sell with full confidence and integrity. The clientele is the best in New Jersey. The co-workers with whom you associate each day have been chosen, each and every one, with the same great care that you have been....The secret that has made L. Bamberger & Co. noted for service, and that has undoubtedly contributed more than any other one factor to make the store, "One of America's Great Stores."[26]

However, on January 19, 1929, Louis Bamberger and his "perfect store" were forever shaken by the sudden death of his partner and brother-in-law Felix Fuld. After developing a cold at the end of December, Fuld succumbed to pneumonia. The loss of a prominent business leader and community champion sent the city of Newark into mourning. "Gone was a city power, a man with strength possibly never equaled in Newark," noted secretary Frank Liveright. "He was noted as 'the best collector' in the city, and charity after charity knew his generous gift and his ability to talk others into large contributions."[27] Fuld's recent $500,000 gift to Newark's Beth Israel Hospital was just one symbol of his generosity. Louis Bamberger never recovered from Fuld's passing. He complained about growing old and did not want to carry the burden of operating the large store on his own.[28] On June 20, 1929, Louis Bamberger entered into negotiations to sell his department store, permanently altering Newark and New Jersey's mercantile life.

Chapter 3

It's Smart to Be Thrifty

B ack in 1913, L. Bamberger & Co. firmly announced that it would never become associated with any other group of retailers. That tradition of independence was the "bulwark" of its success. "The Bamberger store is owned and controlled by its founders. It has no connection with any other store, syndicate, or association. What it chooses to do it does WITHOUT OUTSIDE INTERFERENCE or suggestion. Its policies are its own. This policy of independence has been a powerful factor in the past and it will continue to be in the future."[29] That feeling changed on June 29, 1929, when rumors surfaced that New York's R.H. Macy & Co. had purchased control of Newark's Bamberger's. Louis Bamberger called off his regular morning "team" meeting and left word that the group would assemble later that day. That morning, a Macy executive confirmed the purchase, but Louis Bamberger refused comment. "I have no statement to make. If Macy wants to tell about it, that is up to them."[30] Although some stock shares had become available to co-workers back in 1927, Louis Bamberger, along with his sister Caroline Bamberger Fuld, still had financial control over the store.

R.H. Macy & Co. celebrated the purchase of Bamberger's. It called Bamberger's "one of the outstanding department stores of the country," adding that it occupied "one of the most modern and highly developed department buildings in the country, designed and equipped for a volume much larger than it at present enjoys." Macy's congratulated itself on the acquisition and promised that the business would maintain its unique local character. Louis Bamberger assumed a position on the R.H. Macy & Co.

board of directors along with the honorary title of chairman of the board of the L. Bamberger & Co. department store. Vice-president and secretary Edgar Bamberger remained with the store and stated that he had no interest in leaving the business. "I'm the last of the Bamberger line here now. I'll have to work twice as hard to keep up the pace," said Edgar.[31] Upon the official announcement of the Macy purchase, Louis Bamberger promised that Bamberger's would continue to be a Newark and New Jersey institution and its commitment to good business practices and philanthropy would remain unchanged. "This is a New Jersey institution, tied up with the very fabric of Newark," stated a formal company announcement. "The new owners have a great respect for the management that has built it and plan to continue that management. [We] emphasize that L. Bamberger & Co. will retain the characteristic and the policies that have made it the remarkable store that it is."[32] Neither party released the purchase price, but it was speculated to be at least $25 million, possibly as high as $50 million. In addition to the store, Macy acquired WOR radio and *Charm* magazine. The sale to Macy marked perfect timing for Louis Bamberger and his sister Caroline. Just a few months later, the stock market declines devastated the American economy and threw the country into the Depression. "When Louis Bamberger sold the business, he insisted on cash only and then came the crash," says former Bamberger's chairman Mark Handler. "In the end, Macy's paid a big, big price for Bamberger's."

L. Bamberger & Co. was not R.H. Macy's first acquisition. In early January 1924, Macy purchased a "substantial interest" in Toledo's Lasalle & Koch Company. He followed this with a similar arrangement with Atlanta's Davison-Paxon-Stokes Company on June 14, 1925. According to company documents, the acquisition of Davison-Paxon-Stokes was "the second step in the direction of the plan long cherished of extending Macy's operations beyond New York City.…In both Toledo and Atlanta, we anticipate continuing and increasing success, for both of these communities are growing rapidly, and are centres of progressive populations."[33] Through the 1920s, Macy's slowly increased its stake in the Toledo and Atlanta stores. Unlike Lasalle's and Davison's, Macy's purchased a controlling interest in Bamberger's from the start.

Louis Bamberger set aside $1 million of the sale proceeds as a gift for longtime co-workers. On September 15, 1929, his final day as company leader, Bamberger summoned 235 co-workers to the store's eleventh floor. These workers had served the department store for fifteen or more years and did not include any of the company executives. Bamberger saw this gift as a "gratuity" for their years of service. He also hoped that the workers would use the funds as a form of pension. Co-workers did not know the value of the gift in advance of the meeting, but some amounts were reportedly as high as $10,000. Freed from the active involvement of the department store, Louis Bamberger concentrated his energies on civic projects and further philanthropic giving. On June 7, 1930, Louis and his sister Caroline Bamberger Fuld announced a $5 million endowment gift that founded the Institute for Advanced Study at Princeton University. Caroline Leopold, a descendant of Edgar Bamberger, acknowledges the family's commitment to the institute. "Louis, Edgar and Caroline Fuld were instrumental in setting up the Institute for Advanced Study. They helped bring Albert Einstein to America," says Leopold. "There is film footage of Einstein getting off of the boat with Edgar Bamberger standing right behind him." The Institute for Advanced Study was defined as a "community of scholars" and was designed by the Bambergers to "provide scholars with opportunities for research without burdening them with financial worries."[34] Louis and Caroline served as the institute's initial president and vice-president, respectively, until 1934.

Rowland Hussey Macy founded his fancy dry goods store on December 4, 1858, on New York's Sixth Avenue, just south of Fourteenth Street. Upon the store's opening, he announced to customers, "The whole of New York City, New York State, the whole of the United States, Come On! I can and will supply you all." Numerous failed businesses had formerly occupied that exact location, and many area merchants assumed that Macy would meet a similar fate. Macy was considered "a prudent, energetic, and painstaking merchant…a fair minded man who dealt out even-handed justice to all."[35] He refused to trade on credit. Although Macy's business became extremely successful in its Sixth Avenue and Fourteenth Street location, he predicted that the area centered between Thirty-fourth Street and Forty-second Street would eventually become "the future business heart of this wonderful city."[36] In 1874, Rowland Macy's success caught the attention of Nathan Straus, a well-known New York crockery and porcelain dealer. Straus wanted to do business in what he perceived to be one of the most progressive and successful stores in the city. Macy rented the basement of his store to Straus but died suddenly in 1877. Straus eventually acquired R.H. Macy & Co. from the family heirs ten years later. His brother Isidor joined Nathan in the firm, and the two men turned R.H. Macy into a retail powerhouse. The business moved to Herald Square in 1902. The brothers described their new store as "the largest and most elaborate establishment in the world…

with every known convenience for the comfort of its patrons. [It will be] the greatest shopping centre ever built."[37] Opening in November 1902, the ten-floor Macy store, under Straus family leadership, grew to nineteen stories and covered over two million square feet of floor space by 1930. During that year, approximately 150,000 customers entered the store each day.[38] Although Isidor and his wife, Ida, succumbed during the 1912 *Titanic* sinking, more than six generations of Straus family members controlled R.H. Macy & Co. over time. After the *Titanic* tragedy, Isidor's descendants ended the family business partnership with their uncle Nathan Straus. Isidor's family stayed with R.H. Macy & Co., while Nathan assumed full control of Brooklyn's Abraham and Straus department store.

When Isidor Straus's family acquired L. Bamberger & Co. in 1929, it was promised that no changes would be made to its format. Unlike the New York Macy's store, Bamberger's was initially a carriage trade retailer. Its vast basement store was a later addition to its operation, a necessary move that accommodated Newark's industrial workforce. Former Bamberger executive Marvin Laba states, "Bamberger's had two different customers [for much of its life]. A 'better' customer who was open to higher prices, and a bargain basement customer." As the nation's economy worsened in late 1929, R.H. Macy & Co. revisited Bamberger's business structure. Herbert N. Straus announced in 1930 that Bamberger's needed drastic reorganization in personnel and business methods in order to remain competitive in the Newark market. L. Bamberger & Co. accommodated the higher-end customer along with the thrifty shopper, and Straus made adjustments to that approach. "The [Bamberger's] customer is in no frame of mind to buy freely, especially articles at higher prices." The change in strategy turned Bamberger's into a business that catered to the moderate-income shopper and more to the "masses." R.H. Macy & Co. dropped some exclusive offerings at Bamberger's in exchange for its "Macy's Own Brand" private level merchandise. In 1932, the last family member, Edgar S. Bamberger, left the department store. After a short retirement, Edgar, along with partner Frank W. Packard, purchased Harper's food and department store in Hackensack, New Jersey. The business was renamed Packard-Bamberger & Co. Throughout the 1930s and 1940s, the store was the second-highest volume New Jersey retail operation behind L. Bamberger & Co. In 1935, Edgar once again retired. He continued with his family's philanthropic programs and served on the board of directors at the Institute for Advanced Study.

In most American cities, department stores presented and promoted community traditions, and this was no exception during Newark's

This photograph shows the Bamberger's building after all additions were completed in 1929. The entire structure contained approximately 1,245,000 square feet spread over fourteen stores, in addition to four basement floors. *Courtesy of the Newark Public Library.*

Christmas season. As early as 1899, Santa Claus made regular appearances at Bamberger's and held court in the corner window at Halsey and Washington Streets. In 1900, Uncle Wiggily entertained children at the store's fourth-floor Circusland, which was renamed Fairyland the following season. Santa Claus gave out free picture books to his young visitors, who later visited Fairyland and viewed lifelike figures of Mother Goose, Gulliver, Cinderella and many others. Each year, Bamberger's expanded its Christmas offerings, and in 1902 the store's massive Toydom, with its entire floor of toys, debuted. Bamberger's stated, "All Newark and its suburbs are going to have toys and dolls, if the stock at Bamberger's may be properly distributed."[39] One of Bamberger's greatest holiday traditions was its Thanksgiving Day Parade. Smaller than its company's counterpart in New York City, the event was inaugurated in 1931 and featured "goblins, clowns, Hottentots, apes" in the "grotesque" parade. The route initially started at the Carteret Academy in Orange, traveled down Central Avenue and ended at Bamberger's Market and Washington Street location. Bamberger officials stated that the first parade would include forty grotesque heads, a sixty-two-foot Gulliver balloon, an air-filled elephant and cat and four bands that would "make enough noise to drive the community insane."[40] Newark resident Jeanette Thomas usually attended Bamberger's parade with her mother as it made its way down Market Street. "It was like the New York parade but without the big balloons. There were bands, politicians with their top hats and a big huge papier-mâché turkey. And it was always followed by the real Santa Claus," recalls Thomas. Bamberger's Thanksgiving Day Parade continued for decades, except from 1942 to 1944, when it was cancelled due to war restrictions.

During the Depression, L. Bamberger & Co. experienced sales declines as Newark and the country suffered from low wages and unemployment. Throughout the 1920s and 1930s, Newark's black population steadily grew and, by 1940, accounted for 10 percent of the city's population. Unfortunately, blacks suffered from a "last hired, first fired" policy of employment and added to Newark's high number of relief cases. Skilled

In 1931, Bamberger's inaugurated its Thanksgiving Parade, which became a Newark tradition until 1957. In this 1940 photograph, Jiminy Cricket makes his way down Market Street. *Courtesy of the Newark Public Library.*

Bamberger's employees, dressed as clowns, pulled a float during the 1933 Thanksgiving Parade. *Courtesy of the Newark Public Library.*

workers and other professionals took low-paying WPA jobs just to earn some money. In 1933, Bamberger's sales dropped by over 19 percent, followed by another decrease of 7 percent for 1934. Housing located in the city's Third Ward fell into disrepair, and trolley tracks deteriorated and occasionally caused heavy traffic problems.[41] In February 1932, Bamberger's published its final edition of *Charm* magazine. As fewer upper-income and middle-class customers traveled into the depressed city center, *Charm* became less relevant to the department store's customer base. It fell victim to R.H. Macy's desire to minimize as many expenses as possible.

America's department stores played crucial roles in the country's patriotic war efforts. Thousands of workers were drafted into service, and 175 men from Bamberger's alone were enlisted in 1942. War bonds were sold to raise funds for the military. Sales workers encouraged shoppers to buy these bonds in addition to regular purchases, and stores built elaborate counters and designed festive windows to stimulate sales. In July 1942, Bamberger's played an active role in the national "Retailers for Victory" campaign. Several department stores worked together to sell $1 billion worth of war bonds

Santa makes his way through Bamberger's sixth-floor toy department in December 1938. In this image from the store magazine *Counter Currents*, Santa is accompanied by "toy conscious executives." *Collection of the author.*

In the December 1938 issue of *Counter Currents* magazine, L. Bamberger & Co. paid tribute to its annual Thanksgiving Day Parade. The article stated, "The feminine pulchritude and he-men of the store made up the marchers and float decorations." More than 450 store employees participated in the event. Much of the parade's preparation occurred at the company's Fifth Street Warehouse. Bamberger's parade was a Newark tradition from 1930 until 1957. *Collection of the author.*

and stamps during the entire month. In addition, Bamberger's organized "Whiteout Day," when large stores throughout the state stopped all business at noon for fifteen minutes and only bond and stamp sales were conducted. The war concerned Macy president Jack I. Straus. Production shifts and material scarcities made it difficult for the company to obtain large amounts of goods. "The profits of a department store are dependent primarily upon the volume of its business, which in turn is dependent upon its ability to obtain merchandise," Straus told shareholders. He acknowledged that the stores in Toledo and Atlanta were enjoying war industry payrolls as local factories constantly produced much-needed materials. But the situation was different in Newark. Many of the middle- and upper-income customers who had left the city during the 1930s relied on automobile transportation from their suburban communities. Straus stated, "In Newark, our Bamberger store is in a general area in which very substantial war production has occurred, but Bamberger's has experienced lesser benefits than might have been expected

This image shows a wartime parade heading east on Broad Street, past Military Park. Kresge-Newark, McCrory's, Hearns and Hahne's were some of the city's major retailers along Broad Street. *Courtesy of the Newark Public Library.*

because of governmental restrictions upon automobile traffic as well as public transportation."[42] As the war neared its conclusion, Bamberger's, along with its Macy's parent, announced plans for its employees who were returning home. The department store established a special training program designed to bring these staff members "up to date and accelerate their development within the organization." As the troops returned home from duty, they often enrolled in R.H. Macy & Co.'s famous Executive Training Squad program, which had been established in the late 1920s.

On March 11, 1944, store founder Louis Bamberger passed away from natural causes at age eighty-eight. Even at his advanced age, Louis had frequently traveled from his South Orange home at 602 Center Street to an office at the Newark store. Former store secretary Frank Liveright described Bamberger in the following way: "Although quiet, retiring and with an aversion to the limelight, [he] nonetheless dominated the firm. He shaped the character of the business through his insistence on the highest ethics in dealing with the public, our employees, and our suppliers. Character. That's what Louis Bamberger had in substantial measure." R.H. Macy & Co. president Jack Straus called him "one of America's most distinguished merchants [who] founded and developed a great mercantile establishment which became a symbol of service to practically the whole State of New Jersey." Newark mayor Vincent J. Murphy ordered all flags flown at half-staff for a period of three days. Louis's will left $1 million to Princeton's Institute for Advanced Study, and his extensive collection of paintings was given to the Newark Museum. His collection of autographs of the Declaration of Independence signers was bequeathed to the New Jersey Historical Society. Other institutions designated in Louis Bamberger's will included Beth Israel Hospital, the Welfare Federation of Newark, the YMHA and the Jewish Children's Home.

Only four months after Louis's death, his sister Caroline Bamberger Fuld passed away at her Lake Placid summer home on July 18, 1944, with her sister C. Lavinia Bamberger at her side. A philanthropist, altruist and civic leader in her own right, Fuld had been elected director of the National Council of Jewish Women in 1931 and had championed projects at the Jewish Day Nursery and Neighborhood House in Newark. She had lived with her bachelor brother in New Jersey until his death, and they had worked side by side for many of the family's charitable projects. Both brother and sister had discouraged publicity about their beneficence and often requested anonymity. The department store that bore the family name was a visible contribution to the growth of Newark and North Jersey. Even under the managerial direction of the R.H. Macy & Co. firm, the Bamberger name would forever be associated with New Jersey and its economic, civic and social past.

Chapter 4

Off to Market

After the war, Newark, New Jersey's largest city, bounced back. Its downtown streets teemed with shoppers and population grew, although at a slower rate than the rest of Essex County. The intersection of Broad and Market Streets, also known as "Four Corners," was often hailed as "the busiest corner in America."[43] Over 300,000 people passed through the intersection daily. Numerous department stores and national retailers lined Newark's main downtown streets. "When I arrived in 1940, Newark was a bustling commercial center," states former mayor Kenneth A. Gibson. Automobiles and buses replaced aging trolleys, and the streets were often congested. "Everybody seemed to travel by bus and made Newark seem different from any other place," recalls Gibson. One of downtown's most active bus stops was located at the corner of Market and Halsey Streets, under Bamberger's signature clock. "That clock on the corner was such a meeting place," says Gibson.

"Bamberger's Newark was such a great monolith," says former executive Marvin Laba. "The tenth floor had a quality restaurant with waitresses and white tablecloths. It was a nice place with a nice atmosphere." Former co-worker Larry Davis states, "You could get anything at Bamberger's. It was a tradition in our family to go shopping in downtown Newark. Bamberger's was massive, and I remember that we had to hold hands because the store was so large." Distribution clerk Barry Marko recalls the downtown store as "majestic." "It was a beautiful store made up of marble and stone with huge ceilings." Co-workers recall the buying offices and large employee cafeteria

Above: This photograph shows a holiday scene on Newark's Broad Street in the late 1940s. The historic Trinity and St. Philip's Cathedral in Military Park is located directly across from the Hahne & Co. downtown store. *Courtesy of the Newark Public Library.*

Right: For many years, Newark's official Christmas tree was located at the entrance to Military Park. The tree was placed opposite Kresge and Hearn's and located near Lerner Shops, Wolf's Cut Rate, Schrafft's restaurant and Loew's State Theatre. *Courtesy of the Newark Public Library.*

on the ninth-and-a-half floor—located just three steps up from the rest of the ninth floor—that housed furniture, carpet and bedding. Buyer Ken Allan says the Newark department store was "colossal." Allan describes the tenth-floor restaurant as "reminiscent of Wanamaker's Crystal Room in Philadelphia, with its private banquet rooms and grill room. It was a throwback to when the store was much more upscale, when it was independent." Allen adds, "After World War II, [R.H. Macy & Co.] reorganized Bamberger's into more of a mainstream store. That became our image." Louis Bamberger historian Linda Forgosh concurs: "Bamberger's no longer had the image of the store that Louis Bamberger founded."

During the 1940s, R.H. Macy & Co. continued its expansion throughout the country. In 1940, it experimented with a small, self-service operation in Syracuse, New York. The limited-service Syracuse unit proved unsuccessful and unprofitable and abruptly closed after Christmas 1940. Bamberger's experimented with a Cash & Carry annex that supplemented its basement operation. Its self-service, low-price policy was modeled after the Syracuse experiment and lasted only a few months. Macy targeted department stores that were underperforming but showed increased sales potential. It acquired the Saxon-Cullum store in Augusta, Georgia, in August 1944. Saxon-Cullum had "encouraging prospects for future growth in the community" and was merged into Atlanta's Davison-Paxon store operation.[44] Later that November, Macy purchased Macon's Union Dry Goods Company, which was also merged into Davison-Paxon. In July 1945, Macy reached the West Coast and acquired O'Connor, Moffatt & Co. in San Francisco. Macy praised the store for its "high degrees of customer acceptance and long history of serving the public faithfully and well."[45] The O'Connor, Moffatt name was replaced by "Macy's San Francisco" in October 1947 after the company insisted that over 85 percent of Bay Area customers were in favor of the change.[46] R.H. Macy ended its shopping spree in March 1947 with the purchase of the John Taylor Dry Goods Company in Kansas City. Macy doubled the size of John Taylor's, creating the largest store between St. Louis and San Francisco.[47] It was rebranded as Macy's in October 1949. After the completion of the Kansas City store purchase, R.H. Macy & Co. reorganized its operating structure. By 1948, all affiliate stores, including Bamberger's, operated under the New York corporate office.

After the war, the country enjoyed an economic rebirth that unfortunately had a detrimental effect on many downtown districts, including Newark. Vulnerable downtowns suffered from population loss, expensive and limited automobile parking, inadequate highways and

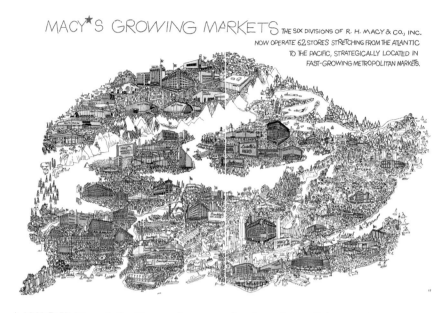

MACY*S GROWING MARKETS THE SIX DIVISIONS OF R. H. MACY & CO., INC. NOW OPERATE 62 STORES STRETCHING FROM THE ATLANTIC TO THE PACIFIC, STRATEGICALLY LOCATED IN FAST-GROWING METROPOLITAN MARKETS.

A 1969 R.H. Macy & Co. illustrated corporate brochure shows all sixty-two Macy company stores located throughout the country. Clockwise from top to the right, the six Macy's divisions were Macy's California (San Francisco), Macy's Missouri-Kansas (Kansas City), Lasalle's (Toledo), Macy's New York (including far-reaching Albany and New Haven locations), Bamberger's (New Jersey) and Davison's (Atlanta). *Collection of the author.*

blighted housing and storefronts.[48] Department stores explored options away from their inner-city flagships. In 1935, Bamberger's experimented with a three-thousand-square-foot women's shop on the Asbury Park Boardwalk. Connected by bridgeway to the Berkeley-Carteret Hotel, Bamberger's called its seasonal Asbury Park shop "One of the most attractive resort stores in the East." Bamberger's made its first true suburban inroads with a small appliance store in East Orange. Opened in April 1945, the East Orange store offered difficult-to-obtain items such as refrigerators, Toastmaster ovens and many kitchen items that showed "definite postwar influence."[49] On December 1, 1947, a Bamberger's appliance and radio center opened in Millburn. Located at 170 Essex Avenue, the ten-thousand-square-foot store was formerly occupied by the Harmony Shop. Inadequate in size, the East Orange store closed in May 1949, and the Millburn location eventually transitioned into a gift boutique and operated well into the 1950s. In January 1948, Bamberger's sold its Newark headquarters building to the Aetna Life Insurance Company for $6.5 million. Bamberger's negotiated a favorable lease-back arrangement for the Newark operation and raised necessary funds for the department store's anticipated suburban growth.

On April 1, 1949, Bamberger's opened a full-line branch operation in Morristown, New Jersey. R.H. Macy president Jack Straus personally selected the location, encouraged by the area's growth and the presence of Bell Laboratories' headquarters. The Morristown store was positioned at Park Place at Speedwell Avenue, the former site of a Schulte-United variety store and National Shoe Store, which were destroyed by fire in September 1945. Bamberger's officials described the Morristown store as "a modern functional arrangement with a background of history, for which the Morris County community is so well known." The Colonial-designed brick store included eight five-foot medallions across the top front of the building. Each medallion represented a famous person associated with Morris County's history, from George Washington to Lewis Morris and Betsy Schuyler. Bamberger's Morristown was located directly across from the Morristown Green, a privately owned common that has always been managed by a

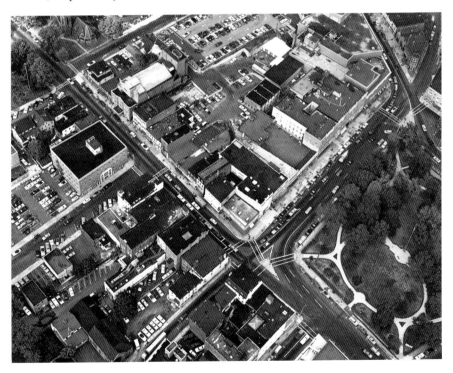

A bird's-eye photograph of downtown Morristown shows the central business district and the Morristown Green. The Bamberger's store is seen in the upper right corner of this image. A small parking lot is located directly behind the store. *Courtesy of the Newark Public Library.*

Bamberger's first full-line branch opened in downtown Morristown on April 1, 1949. The company called the branch "Morris County's newest and most exciting new store." Bamberger's three-story air-conditioned location contained everything for "your whole family and home." *Courtesy of the New Jersey Historical Society.*

board of trustees. "The secret to Morristown is the Green," says historian Margaret Brady. Brady calls Morristown "a microcosm of the United States, and the Green is part of the community's identity." Thousands of customers attended the store's grand opening. "Crowds pressed solidly from counter to counter and wall to wall," according to news reports.[50] Originally, the store advertised dainty Princess Aloha Hawaiian orchids as its opening day giveaway, but a sudden federal import ban changed plans. The flowers were found to carry Oriental fruit fly larvae, a potentially dangerous insect pest. Instead, gardenias, along with carnations and snapdragons, were given to the first group of female customers. Bamberger's gave away ten thousand gardenias within the first half hour alone. John C. Williams, Bamberger's president, proclaimed that the new Morristown store "will save our customers the extensive trip to Newark and at the same time make available to them the same Bamberger service and wide range of selection to be expected of a large store."[51] However, some local customers were underwhelmed with the new branch store. "The stores in Morristown didn't quite impress me," states Margaret Brady. "As a child, we'd go to the Newark [Bamberger's] for an Easter outfit or a dress. Newark was my kind of store. I grew up in Brooklyn, and we had the big department stores." Brady continues, "Bamberger's Morristown seemed stagnant. The same things were always in the same place. And it just wasn't a classy-looking building." Bamberger's Morristown store received stiff competition from M. Epstein, a local department store founded in 1912. Its five-story, 110,000-square-foot building was located on Park Place opposite the Morristown Green. "Epstein's always had a little more personality than Bamberger's," recalls Brady. "Their service was a little more specialized, and it employed many local longtime people." Former Morristown employee Larry Davis remembers Bamberger's Morristown as "a family store. It was really a fun place. Watching the store evolve throughout the seasons, from spring, summer and fall, was really something. When I got drafted, they had a [going-away] party for me on every floor." One of the city's great holiday traditions occurred at the Bamberger's store. "Morristown had one Santa, and he lived in a house on the Green," says Brady. "He would arrive on the weekend after Thanksgiving. Bamberger's had a flat roof, and he always showed up on its roof, where he was escorted down by firefighters. There were spotlights and thousands of people. Santa was escorted to the Green, where he flicked a switch and turned on the Christmas lights."

By 1950, WOR had become a burden on R.H. Macy & Co. As radio and television technology advanced, the cost of operating the corporation under the Macy umbrella affected the bottom line of the entire department store business. Since its beginning in 1922, WOR had operated under the name Bamberger Broadcasting Service, Incorporated. On October 5, 1949, WOR-TV made its on-air debut, and the broadcasting corporation

Opens Monday 9:45 a.m.
Plainfield's NEW Bam's

When Bamberger's opened its Plainfield branch on May 10, 1954, it proudly advertised "modern-as-airliner fixtures, long sweeping aisles, kindly vivid lighting, and clean conditioned air." The new branch included a gourmet shop, gift shop, optical shop and bakeshop. The lower level contained an entire city block of home furnishings. *Collection of the author.*

was renamed General Teleradio, Inc. The new name reflected the increased investment in WOR by General Tire & Rubber Company. However, R.H. Macy & Co. told shareholders that "earnings were affected adversely by the unfavorable operating results of the radio and television subsidiary, because of the cost of television operations at this stage of its development."[52] Once an important piece of the Bamberger empire, Macy sold the radio and television station to General Tire & Rubber in October 1951. Edgar Bamberger, Louis's nephew and former store secretary, was the president of WOR. His passing on June 29, 1952, just eight months after the sale of WOR, marked an official end to the Bamberger family retail era.

On May 10, 1954, L. Bamberger & Co. opened its second full-line suburban branch store, in Plainfield, New Jersey. Located on East Front Street and Roosevelt Avenue, the 133,000-square-foot Plainfield location was billed as "a complete department store in miniature" that would carry a "representative cross-section of the more than 400,000 items to be found at Bamberger's Newark."[53] The store included a replica of the Newark store's Mirror Room, which stocked the company's "high style fashions." The Plainfield Mirror Room had the same Italian design as the Newark salon, with starburst chandeliers and gold mirrored panels. The Plainfield store was merchandised along the lines of the Newark flagship, except for a bargain basement, but promised a change of merchandise "if a preferential trend develops in the community."[54] Bamberger's Plainfield was located a few blocks from the city center. Its strongest competitor was Tepper's, founded in 1907, which adopted the slogan "Central Jersey's Shopping Center." Plainfield historian Nancy Piwowar says, "Bamberger's was more

In May 1954, Bamberger's was "tickled pink to be in Plainfield" with its newest branch store. The Plainfield store was designed with many of the architectural elements of the Morristown location. This photograph shows the Roosevelt Avenue side of the building during the store's opening days. *Courtesy of the Newark Public Library.*

modern than Tepper's, but Tepper's was more upscale. Tepper's was a taller building with a mezzanine and elevators with operators and gates." Somerville resident Jeanne Locke recalls dressing her children on Saturday mornings and loading them into a station wagon for shopping trips into Plainfield. "Tepper's was a step up in quality and value from Bamberger's," says Locke. "I loved the character of Tepper's. They had a dress maker and tailors on hand to make alterations if needed, and the staff was very friendly and helpful. We would spend the morning at Tepper's and be there into the afternoon." But Bamberger's proved to be a formidable competitor to Tepper's. Bamberger's offered expanded merchandise selections at its Plainfield store. Piwowar remembers two distinct departments at the Plainfield location: "I remember getting off of the escalator and seeing a department called 'Chubette,' and I was so thankful I didn't have to go there. The store also had a liquor department with a separate entrance. We often had liquor delivered to the house from Bamberger's, and we thought, as kids, that it seemed so upscale." Piwowar says that people in Plainfield usually knew that Bamberger's was a

Construction of the sixty-thousand-square-foot Bamberger's store at the Princeton Shopping Center commenced in May 1951. The moderately sized store consisted of a "cross section of complete lines carried by the Newark store." The Princeton Bamberger's was completed in September 1954. *Collection of the Historical Society of Princeton.*

part of Macy's. "We knew Macy's from the parade and from *Miracle on 34th Street*. We thought that it was so cool that Plainfield had a Macy's." Shortly after the Plainfield store's opening, Bamberger's opened another branch, this time at the Princeton Shopping Center. The compact two-story, sixty-thousand-square-foot store opened on September 9, 1954. It was the company's first shopping center location. Located on Barrison Street, just a mile from the center of town, Bamberger's carried a more limited selection than was found in the Morristown and Plainfield branches. Although it was smaller and farther from the headquarters store, officials "always had a soft spot for the Princeton store," states former president Rudolph J. Borneo. "It was tiny, very small, but everybody loved it," states another former president, Mark S. Handler.

In 1954, the company officially changed the store name from L. Bamberger & Co. to Bamberger's. Marvin Laba worked as a stockboy in the Newark store and even remembers seeing Louis Bamberger come through the store one day. He was "a small man who was bent over a little." Even as a child, Laba knew that "small man" was a retailing legend and an incredible philanthropist. Laba originally regretted the name change to Bamberger's. "It was always L. Bamberger & Co. The name was a tradition; it sounded like it belonged. 'Bamberger's' just sounded strange." Many residents and customers didn't even call the store Bamberger's; they simply called it Bam's.

Chapter 5

Broad and Market

A lthough it was billed as "New Jersey's Greatest Store," Bamberger's, or Bam's, was certainly not the only department store that called the Garden State home. Department stores such as Dunham's, Yards and Swern's in Trenton; Hurley's and Kotlikoff's in Camden; Steinbach Company in Asbury Park; Goerke in Elizabeth; and M.E. Blatt in Atlantic City were only part of New Jersey's large field of local department store retailers. Louis Bamberger often said that "competition is good," and as the department store industry developed, Newark and New Jersey became a very competitive market.

HAHNE & COMPANY

Founded in 1858 by Julius Hahne and partner Adam Block, Hahne & Co. was regarded as Newark's signature "carriage-trade" department store. Born in Saxony, Germany, Hahne traveled to Newark and worked in a leather factory before he saved $500 and opened his own storefront. When it opened on Central Avenue, Hahne & Block was advertised as a "Toy and Fancy Goods" operation. It originally sold only canary birds but soon expanded to pocketbooks, notions, yard goods, linens and home furnishings.[55] Hahne & Block encouraged potential shoppers to "Walk In and Look Around." From the start, Hahne & Block offered home delivery, first by wheelbarrows and

Pedestrians and buses crowded the intersection of Broad and Market Streets in 1957. Many longtime Newarkers affectionately referred to the busy intersection as "Four Corners." *Collection of the Newark Public Library.*

later by wagon and trucks. In later years, Hahne & Co. claimed to be the city's first store to establish fixed price tags that eliminated bargaining and haggling.[56] Block sold his interest in 1871, and Hahne expanded the business and gradually purchased land along Broad Street. He passed away in 1895 before his grand emporium, with "100 stores under one roof," was built.

The 465,000-square-foot Hahne & Co. building opened for business on September 3, 1901. It featured a 200-foot-deep, 108-foot-tall Grand Court; fifty show windows; ten passenger elevators; and a 106-foot-long onyx "magnificent soda fountain" and employed 1,200 workers. The four-story brick and terra-cotta building was promoted as "the only thoroughly fire-proof mercantile structure in New Jersey." Hahne & Co.'s adopted slogan was "New Jersey's Greatest Store with the Smallest Prices."[57] In 1925, as part of the company's "rehabilitation and beautification," its impressive Grand Court was filled in.[58] It added 15,000 square feet of floor space in an area where "only radio waves and winged things could travel before."[59] In 1931, Hahne & Co. was acquired by the new holding company Associated Dry Goods.

Though intended to be a "People's Store," Hahne's, located on the other end of Newark's central business district from Bamberger's, attracted older, affluent, conservative customers.[60] Former Bamberger's president Rudolph J. Borneo says, "At Hahne's, you got caught up in the past, not the future. Hahne's was old school; it never really evolved." Newark resident Jeanette Thomas recalls how during her youth, the Hahne's saleswomen "wore stark white shirts and long black dresses with gloves." In 1929, Hahne's moved into North Jersey's suburbs, well before its local competitors, with a small store in Montclair. It was replaced in February 1951 with "an adventure in suburban selling." The building was sanitized by a glycol vapor–dispensing device that filled the airspace and caused "a virtual massacre of bacteria and virus."[61] On March 12, 1963, Hahne's expanded into Westfield with a complete Georgian-style department store that offered "fashion, quality, and good taste." Hahne & Co. did not expand any further outside its stores in Newark, Montclair and Westfield until 1972.

KRESGE-NEWARK

L. Simon Plaut and Leopold Fox opened a small novelty dry goods store in 1870. The business, named Fox & Plaut, followed a one-price policy and continually expanded. Plaut's two brothers, Louis and Moses, joined the business shortly after the store's founding. After Fox passed away, the store assumed the name The Bee Hive and was "the largest dry and fancy goods house in New Jersey."[62] The Plaut store developed an early mutual aid association for its employees, and a large number of store executives were promoted within the store's ranks. By the early 1920s, L.S. Plaut & Co. had swelled to more than one thousand employees and 100,000 square feet of space.

On July 30, 1923, Sebastian S. Kresge, the famous variety merchant, purchased the L.S. Plaut & Co. store on Newark's Broad Street for $17 million. Kresge envisioned a national chain of large department stores, and his acquisition of L.S. Plaut & Co. afforded him that possibility.[63] S.S. Kresge and L. Simon Plaut issued a joint statement: "The Plaut name has always stood first for integrity. It will be of the new organization to maintain that

Kresge purchased the L.S. Plaut & Co. store in 1923 and made major alterations and expansions to the building. The right side of this photograph shows the rear of the Goerke store, which sold out to Hearn's and S. Klein in later years. *Courtesy of the Newark Public Library.*

reputation." The statement continued: "Contemplated building plans will enable the Plaut store to live up to its slogan, 'The Store of Personal Service.'" Kresge immediately embarked on an expansion plan to rebuild. Construction began in August 1924 on a new nine-story department store designed by the New York firm Starrett Brothers. The brick and stone structure of "modified renaissance design" would house 700,000 square feet. The $2.5 million structure opened in sections, and the building celebrated its completion on September 8, 1926. Despite the original purchase agreement specifying that the Plaut name would be preserved, the company had officially changed the store name to Kresge-Newark by the end of 1926. Kresge-Newark operated as a separate entity from Kresge's five-and-ten stores, and it was managed for years by the charitable Kresge Foundation.

S.S. Kresge expanded his new department store experiment and purchased Washington's Palais Royal and Asbury Park's Steinbach Company. The Kresge-Newark operation opened small satellite locations

Until 1964, Kresge-Newark was one of Newark's Big Three department stores. The prominent Broad Street landmark served largely middle-income customers who traded between Bamberger's and Hahne's. The business was sold to David Chase and renamed until discounter Two Guys purchased the lease in 1968. *Courtesy of the Newark Public Library.*

in Summit and East Orange. Kresge-Newark became a shopping destination for those who did not want the merchandise depth and value at Bamberger's and the higher prices and persnickety atmosphere at Hahne's. As a former Bamberger president, Rudolph J. Borneo remembers Kresge-Newark as "just another retailer in the city. They did their own thing. We [Bamberger's] didn't look at them as significant." Former Newark resident and Bamberger's buyer Ken Allan feels otherwise: "Kresge was such a unique store. It was a very well-rounded store. It was more upper-end than Bamberger's. They had a full-service dining room with a full bar service." Allan saw Kresge as a "fun store." Its popular Breakfast with Santa event was a Newark tradition. After World War II, Kresge-Newark installed a monorail, manufactured by the Louden Machinery Company, along the ceiling of its ninth-floor toy department. But in 1959, Kresge-Newark leased the top two floors of its store to Western Electric, and the monorail ride came to an end. In April 1964, Kresge-Newark was sold to Hartford businessman David T. Chase for $8 million. The Kresge Foundation was interested in selling the department store to "allow some diversification of the foundation's assets in enterprises other than merchandising." Chase enthusiastically pledged himself to the department store and promised increased quality and services, in addition to a new name, Chase-Newark. The purchase by Chase proved a burden on the businessman's finances. "With Chase, it still looked like Kresge, but [Chase] wanted to take it up a notch," says Allan. "It was a very expensive proposition." Just after Christmas 1967, Chase announced that the department store, reduced in size since the Kresge days, was closing in February 1968. The middle-class customers who had supported the Chase store had stopped making regular excursions into the struggling downtown shopping district. When Chase closed its doors, approximately eight hundred workers, many hired during the Kresge-Newark era, were out of jobs.

OHRBACH'S, HEARN'S AND KLEIN'S

Between the 1930s and 1970s, three separate retailers from New York's Union Square set up shop in downtown Newark. All of these businesses catered to value-oriented customers, and some had longer tenures than others. But all three stores helped strengthen downtown Newark as New Jersey's premier shopping destination.

In 1923, Nathan Ohrbach opened a women's apparel store that was famous for selling lower-priced clothing than typical department stores. With the slogan "A business in millions, a profit in pennies," Ohrbach's offered $1.00 and $5.00 dresses and became well known for its copies of French designer apparel. In July 1930, it assumed the long-term lease of the former Bamberger's store, also known as Bamberger's Annex, at Market and Halsey Streets. By 1937, Ohrbach's had expanded its store four times, installed new elevators and escalators and utilized the entire seven-story former Bamberger store. Ohrbach's was a downtown Newark fixture for forty-three years. "Why would you buy a dress at Bamberger's for $19.99 when you could buy the same dress at Ohrbach's for $12.99?" asks Newark resident Jeanette Thomas. The value-oriented department store closed on January 31, 1974, after a decade of sales declines and the inability to secure a better leasing arrangement. Upon Ohrbach's closure announcement, Bamberger's Newark manager Richard Leeds stated, "I would like to assure you personally that [Bamberger's] has no intention whatsoever of closing our Newark store…and we will continue to serve the Newark community enthusiastically and well as we have since 1893."[64] After the Newark store closure, Ohrbach's operated stores at the Bergen Mall, Willowbrook Mall and Woodbridge Center until 1986.

"There's no place like Hearn's for Value!" proclaimed the department store in 1914. George A. Hearn founded his store on New York's Canal Street in 1827. In 1879, Hearn's moved to Fourteenth Street, and by the 1920s, the small notions store had grown into a 700,000-square-foot business that employed almost 3,000 workers. The store left family hands in 1932 and shifted to a format of lower prices with limited services. When the R.J. Goerke & Sons store at 689 Broad Street became available in 1937, Hearn's opened its Newark branch and operated under the New York store's management. Over 20,000 shoppers visited Hearn's-Newark on opening day, with police and firemen on hand to control the crowds. The nine-story department store employed 750 workers and housed high-speed escalators that had "a capacity 15 times that of the average escalator." Mayor Ellenstein declared that Hearn's would "usher in a new era in Newark's mercantile life" and credited the company for its "ambition, foresight, and business acumen."[65] However, management troubles and operating losses at the main New York store limited the success of the Newark branch, and it eventually closed in 1949.

In February 1950, S. Klein on the Square, another New York Union Square retailer, opened in the 220,000-square-foot recently closed Hearn's

Macy's New York division lists some of its earlier locations in this corporate brochure. Aside from Herald Square, the stores listed (from top to bottom) are Roosevelt Field (1956), White Plains (1949), Flatbush (1948), Jamaica (1947) and Parkchester (1941). As of 2016, the Parkchester Macy's is still in operation. *Collection of the author.*

store. S. Klein was a pioneer in the discount department store industry and provided shoppers a chaotic atmosphere that included tables of quality bargains. Its tagline, "On the Square," was a pun that combined its main Union Square location with an expression that means "honest and aboveboard." "S. Klein was always a lower-end store, but it was busy! An announcer was always barking out the latest bargains on a PA system, and you could watch this person on the balcony level," recalls former resident Ken Allan. Ironically, S. Klein Newark was not a victim of its aging store's infrastructure but rather its parent company. The Rapid-American Corporation transitioned the promotional bargain department store into a stagnant and vague retailer. The Newark S. Klein store, with its signature signage, closed in June 1975, but its prominent building, opposite Military Park, was left untouched for decades and was a shuttered reminder of the shopping mecca that Newark once was.

New York department store Oppenheim, Collins was a pioneer in the New Jersey market. From 1909 to 1929, it operated a four-story small department store at Broad and Williams Streets in Newark. Unable to carry a full selection of merchandise, it closed its doors. In the 1940s, it reestablished its presence with branches in East Orange, Morristown and Hackensack.

On March 30, 1931, East Orange became home to B. Altman & Co., a Fifth Avenue carriage trade retailer. Located on Central Avenue, the three-story store carried "a complete line of merchandise and served customers living in the Oranges and adjacent communities."[66] When B. Altman & Co. moved to Short Hills in 1956, it found itself in an ever-growing field of fine exclusive New York retailers, such as Saks Fifth Avenue, Franklin Simon and Lord & Taylor, that were making their marks in the Garden State.

Chapter 6

Everything Changed with Paramus

With over two hundred departments spread over nine selling floors and a two-level basement store, Bamberger's Newark store was the quintessential big-city department store. As former store manager Rudolph J. Borneo recalls, "When I came to Bamberger's in 1954, the Newark store had a real sense of history and was still doing business." Borneo was a member of the store's Executive Training Squad, and his first sales experience involved a White Sale. "I brought out towels from the stock room, and I never made it to the table. [Shoppers] took every one out of my hands." The scene was not much different in the basement during special events. Store officials immediately discontinued one particular sale when approximately one thousand women, and some men, became unmanageable. "The noise and confusion became too much for the harassed sales force," stated an article in the *New York Times*. "Several women complained of feeling ill and one or two fainted. Others indignantly accused them of staging their swoons for the purpose of obtaining priority."[67] Former resident Marilyn Rosen fondly remembers shopping at the downtown Newark Bamberger's. "The store was just so crowded. Everybody was there. [Living in Irvington,] it was the big city to us. And at the end, my friends and I would always meet up at the clock." Borneo adds, "The Newark store had a real vibrancy to it [in the 1950s], but obviously over the years, that deteriorated."

One of the first cultural changes at the Newark flagship store occurred in 1955, when the ornate tenth-floor restaurant closed its doors. The loss of Bamberger's public restaurant eliminated a dining and social option for its middle- to upper-income clientele. The only other food options in the department store were several snack bars located throughout the store and the Dinette lunch counter on the first basement level. Bamberger's established a long-term lease of its tenth-floor restaurant location with the Downtown Club, Newark's oldest private dining club. The Downtown Club catered to high-power downtown business works and was "a social gathering place for much of northern New Jersey."[68]

The year 1957 was the final one of Bamberger's Newark Thanksgiving Parade. Held primarily on a half-mile trotting track at Weequahic Park, it was carried live on ABC-TV across the country. The event had become a Thanksgiving Eve Parade in an effort to not compete with its parent store's Macy's Thanksgiving Parade in New York City. When Bamberger's dropped its Newark parade plans in 1958, President David L. Yunich announced a statewide "Universal Christmas" in its place. Festivities in celebration of the United Nations would be observed in all Bamberger's stores. Yunich stated, "Surveys show us that in recent years more and more families have watched

Bamberger's upscale tenth-floor restaurant catered to some of the store's higher-end clientele. The large formal dining facility was discontinued in 1955. In 1936, the restaurant featured murals of New Jersey maps, which dated from 1806. *Courtesy of the Newark Public Library.*

the parade on television, rather than along the parade route. This was true whether the parade was held in the daytime or at night. Since there are other televised Thanksgiving parades available to the people of this area, and since the universal Christmas will hold much meaning for the people of our state, we felt that we could step out of the picture this year without harming the public interest."

When former president David Yunich began his tenure in 1955, Bamberger's was R.H. Macy's least profitable division. Yunich found a "vast, down-at-the-heels main store in Newark, sitting forlornly in a decaying area where urban blight had hurt retail business and discouraged shoppers."[69] The massive Newark flagship was supported by only a few undersized branch stores, two that were located in small urban downtown districts. The northern New Jersey suburbs were growing at an incredible rate, becoming bedroom communities for New York City and Newark commuters. By the mid-1950s, Newark was the country's "most commuted-to" major city, and its daytime population was twice the size of its evening number.[70] Yunich assessed Bamberger's situation and told executives that the division's future was not dependent on a turnaround of the Newark store. Instead, its future was in the suburbs. Yunich announced, "I don't want to set the world on fire, I want to set New Jersey on fire." The comment baffled Macy executives, but Yunich said, "I'm convinced that the real future for Bam's isn't in the revival of the Newark store. I know that is what you and Jack [Straus, R.H. Macy & Co. president] charged me with. But after some experience there now, there's no way you can do that and have it mean anything. But there is a way to go that will have some real clout, and that is to capitalize on the great Bamberger name by taking it all over the state of New Jersey."[71]

In November 1951, when R.H. Macy & Co. purchased a thirty-acre plot of land at the intersection of Highways 4 and 17, Paramus was known as the "Celery Capital of the World." "There were a lot of farms and wooded areas [in Paramus]," says Bill Leaver, curator at the Fritz Behnke History Museum. "The farmers were not making money off of their crops, so they were selling off their land to developers." Located in Bergen County, Paramus and its immediate surrounding communities enjoyed a higher-than-average annual family income, as well as proximity to many accessible highways. In 1953, the R.H. Macy & Co. headquarters announced plans for the Garden State Plaza Shopping Center. The $25 million Garden State Plaza was the department store group's first shopping center and was part of a wholly owned company subsidiary named the Garden State Plaza Corporation. Garden State Plaza was designed to be built in four sections and potentially

In 1951, the R.H. Macy corporation purchased land along Route 4 in Bergen County. However, Macy corporate officials wanted to operate the Paramus store as a Macy's, not Bamberger's. Macy officials felt Route 4 was a main roadway that drew residents and customers into New York City. After three years of debate between the two divisions, Bamberger's convinced the parent corporation that it was best suited to operate the Paramus store. *Collection of the author.*

grow to 1.5 million square feet. R.H. Macy & Co. stated that the new center would be anchored by a Macy's department store, controlled by the management of the Macy's New York division. The parent company had never operated a Macy's branded store in New Jersey. Although New Jersey was Bamberger's territory, Macy's corporate headquarters felt "the site was historically more tributary to New York than Newark in shopping traffic, highway system, commuter buses, train service pattern, and newspaper coverage."[72] Bamberger officials were angered by the decision and in 1954 finally convinced corporate headquarters that the new Paramus store should exist as a Bamberger store. Jack I. Straus, R.H. Macy & Co. president, stated, "The new branch will be part of the Bamberger operation instead of the Macy chain as previously announced because the New York store already has so many branches in operation."[73]

Macy's, Bamberger's parent company, was unaware that the Allied Stores Corporation had also purchased land in the immediate area. Allied was the parent of Stern's, a one-time carriage trade retailer on New York's Forty-second Street that had evolved into a moderately priced department store. Once the two retail corporations became aware of each other's intentions,

Automobiles begin to fill the parking lot on opening day at Bamberger's Garden State Plaza store. The first phase of the center, which included the Bamberger's store, opened on May 1, 1957. *Courtesy of the Newark Public Library.*

they investigated combining both projects into one massive shopping complex. However, a dispute over landownership rights was compounded by a stream that separated both parcels. Allied and Macy's parted ways and continued with separate shopping center plans. The Bergen Mall was constructed just seven-eighths of a mile east of the Garden State Plaza along Route 17. The two shopping centers appealed to the same middle-class demographic, and both centers brought over two million square feet of retailing to the former marshy woodland in Paramus. Critics doubted that both centers could be profitable and thought "each center [was] likely to emerge with weaker tenant relations." One area realtor claimed that the two centers "competing as they are with the same merchandise and same service, are ridiculous separately." Garden State Plaza opened in May 1957, while the Bergen Mall opened just six months later in November 1957. The two shopping centers engaged in a rivalry that increased annual retail sales in Paramus from $5 million in 1949 to close to $125 million in 1959.

After its initial 1957 opening, the Garden State Plaza in Paramus remained in a constant state of construction and expansion. Despite being an active construction zone, the plaza greatly exceeded all sales expectations. *Collection of the author.*

A futuristic canopy was part of the original architectural design of Bamberger's Garden State Plaza store. A Bamberger's shoppers' parking shuttle bus is parked outside the canopy in this 1957 photograph. *Courtesy of the Newark Public Library.*

Above: Bamberger's Garden State Plaza store promoted "do-it-yourself delivery" and encouraged shoppers to take their packages home upon purchase. As the era of department store home delivery services came to a close, retailers like Bamberger's hoped that bringing home purchases by automobile would help in the "togetherness of family shopping." *Collection of the author.*

Below: Garden State Plaza was designed as a "cluster-type shopping center," with Bamberger's as the largest suburban branch store in the northeastern United States. For its first thirty years, Garden State Plaza was an outdoor shopping complex. *Collection of the author.*

The sheer size of the Garden State Plaza Bamberger's store set it apart from its other branches. Bamberger's Paramus opened with 340,000 square feet in space, more than three times the size of its Plainfield branch and almost six times larger than the two-level Princeton Shopping Center branch. A full-line basement store with Bamberger's signature "Aisle of Savings" from the Newark store was reported to be the first complete basement operation in a branch department store. It was slightly larger than the neighboring Bergen Mall Stern's store, but both stores were much larger than suburban department store branches of the past. These branches were often criticized as "too small to reflect the true character of the parent store, and their appeal was limited."[74] This was not true at Bamberger's Paramus. "The real success was that it was a mega store. It proved that you could do substantial business at a branch store," recalls former president Marvin Laba. Former president Mark S. Handler says Bamberger's Paramus "changed the equation. We had this giant, huge Paramus store but we also had some small locations like Morristown and Plainfield." The two types of stores taught the corporation that branch stores should be operated individually. The store's strength and popularity in Paramus supported Yunich's vision that Bamberger's future was in the suburbs, not the city. Unlike Macy's branches in New York or Marshall Field's locations throughout Chicago, Bamberger's suburban success was not reliant on Newark's vision or fashion trends. "Bamberger's became very focused on our individual stores and customers because we did not have a main store [Newark] that drove our buyers and merchandisers," says Handler. Executive Rudolph Borneo calls Paramus the "catalyst." "The demographic showed enormous growth, and our management team was always pushing the Bamberger stores to the next level," states Borneo.

Building on the success of Paramus, Bamberger's marched forward into New Jersey's suburbs. Its future was based on large branch stores in progressive shopping centers. The company made some adjustments to its current business to maintain its momentum. In September 1957, Yunich announced the closure of the small Millburn store. Millburn initially operated as an appliance outlet but transitioned into a gift and accessories store in 1955. Yunich stated that Millburn "was not representative of a Bamberger store and [was] too small to meet the needs of our customers."[75] On the other hand, in 1958, Bamberger's released plans to double the size of its Morristown store and increase the store's parking facilities by 1961.

Bamberger's opened its 291,000-square-foot store at the Menlo Park Shopping Center on September 1, 1959. Edison's mayor cut the ribbon with golden shears and a company official released one thousand doves,

Stern's Bergen Mall store featured a large glass frontage along its plaza entry. The mall's main courtyard often featured special events such as fashion shows and band concerts. *Courtesy of the Newark Public Library.*

Stern Brothers of New York announced the development of a "sister store" at Paramus's new Bergen Mall in 1954. The rendering shows the proposed store by Stern's parent, Allied Stores Corporation. Allied, developer of the shopping center, planned a 300,000-square-foot Stern's, along with one hundred smaller stores. A 1957 opening was planned. *Collection of the author.*

symbolizing peace and goodwill toward its local citizens. Ten thousand opening day customers were "greeted by hostesses in costumes of foreign nations."[76] The new Menlo Park center contained about sixty stores and provided parking for approximately six thousand cars. At the time of Menlo Park's opening, R.H. Macy & Co. claimed some hardship. Expenses at the new Davison's store in Lenox Square in suburban Atlanta also adversely affected the parent company's corporate earnings. The Menlo Park and Lenox Square stores quickly established their clientele and became some of the corporation's leading performers. Menlo Park was the only Bamberger's location, other than Paramus and Newark, that housed a full basement store operation. Former employee Barry Marko remembers the Menlo Park store at Christmastime and the bells and chimes that were located on the roof. Menlo Park enjoyed a loyal customer base and staff, and its popularity proved that the company was headed toward a path of prosperity and retail dominance.

Bamberger's purchased forty-three acres of farmland at the Eatontown traffic circle in 1954. Even as the company celebrated the Menlo Park opening, construction continued in this new location in Monmouth County. The Monmouth Shopping Center opened on March 1, 1960, with Bamberger's as its leading tenant. A total of 100,000 customers visited the center on

Bamberger's was an original anchor at the Menlo Park Shopping Center, along with Montgomery Ward and the Arcadian Gardens nursery. The center opened on September 1, 1959. Just six months later, Bamberger's opened another location at the Monmouth Shopping Center in Eatontown. Both Bamberger stores loosely featured similar architectural details. This image shows an aerial view of the Menlo Park Center. *Collection of the author.*

opening day, and the Eatontown mayor helped release three thousand helium-filled balloons as part of the celebration. "Monmouth was a good size store that served a wonderful shore area population," says Handler. The Menlo Park and Monmouth Bamberger's each featured a popular liquor department, along with a small bar. Drive-in auto centers were operated by the department store in Menlo Park and Monmouth, as well as Paramus, Plainfield and downtown Newark. A special forty-thousand-square-foot auto center and furniture clearance outlet was situated on Route 22 in Springfield. The Monmouth Shopping Center store was located approximately forty-five minutes from the Newark headquarters. Former executive Marvin Laba remembers Monmouth as "a good store," but back in 1960, "it seemed like it was quite far away."

"The success of Bamberger's was with the leadership," says Borneo. After the opening of Bamberger's Garden State Plaza location, the Bamberger's division, under the leadership of David Yunich, saw annual sales grow from a meager $80 million to over $500 million. Macy's New York ultimately wanted Yunich to join its division as president. However, Yunich was happy at Bamberger's and reluctant to cross the Hudson River. R.H. Macy & Co. president Jack I. Straus refused to leave Yunich in Newark. "We are going to use you here [at Macy's New York]. You've done your job there [at Bamberger's]," said Straus. Herbert L. Seegal, a vice-president of merchandise at Macy's New York division, replaced David Yunich in Newark.[77] Seegal brought Ed Finkelstein, New York merchandise administrator, to join him at Bamberger's. It was the start of a managerial team that changed the face of Bamberger's. Seegal and Finkelstein felt that there was plenty of work to do at Bamberger's. "Bam's was still an ordinary, staid, old-fashioned type of department store group," said Seegal. They decided to give each Bamberger's store the power to make its own buying decisions, carry merchandise specific to the local customer and create elaborate displays that represented goods in exciting and unusual formats. With the successful combination of Seegal and Finkelstein at the helm in Newark, R.H. Macy & Co. cited Bamberger's as "one of Macy's most vital, progressive, prosperous, and promising divisions."[78]

Rudolph Borneo says, "The executives at Bamberger's built a very strong business. Herb Seegal was an incredible leader and teacher. He taught constantly. I remember when I was a sales manager in Monmouth and Herb was walking through, asking questions like 'what was selling, etc.?' Ed was a genius and was so loyal to the people. He was a visionary." Philip Schlein joined Bamberger's as a senior vice-president of merchandising. "He was

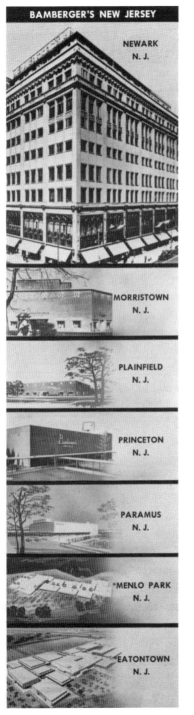

BAMBERGER'S NEW JERSEY

NEWARK
N. J.

MORRISTOWN
N. J.

PLAINFIELD
N. J.

PRINCETON
N. J.

PARAMUS
N. J.

MENLO PARK
N. J.

EATONTOWN
N. J.

a strong merchant, very creative," recalls Borneo. Marvin Laba calls Phil Schlein an "extremely good people person." On one occasion, Laba approached Schlein at his office. He told him that he wanted to talk to him about not being promoted. "Phil picked up the phone, called his wife and said that he couldn't meet her for dinner. I told him that we could carry this on tomorrow, but Phil said he could skip dinner." R.H. Macy president Jack I. Straus did not play a visible role at Bamberger's. Straus served on the board of all Macy's divisions, but "we never felt his presence," says Borneo. "He obviously had an influence on some directors. It was Herb Seegal and Ed Finkelstein who really impacted our lives."

Both Borneo and Laba served on Bamberger's Executive Training Squad. The Executive Training Squad dated back to 1927, when Macy's New York developed the early business acceleration program. "The Training Squad program consists of carefully planned training in the major disciplines of the retail business," stated a 1964 company document.[79] The program trainees received classroom instruction and participated in lectures, conferences, workshops and on-the-job experience "to

In 1960, Bamberger's listed its locations, in order of oldest to youngest, in an R.H. Macy Annual Report. With the flagship Newark store prominently positioned on top, the branch stores were Morristown (1949), followed by Plainfield (1954), Princeton (1954), Paramus (1957), Menlo Park (1960) and Monmouth (1960). *Collection of the author.*

provide a broad understanding of the business." Trainees received frequent evaluations and were notified of their strengths and weaknesses. "My first assignment was as a trainee in toys," remembers Marvin Laba. "That [Newark toy] department operated with precision. [As trainees,] sometimes we would work as late as 3:00 a.m. and be expected back by 7:00 or 8:00 a.m. the next morning. You never worked harder in your life." When Laba started in the Training Squad, one boss told a group of trainees, "If you have a girlfriend or wife, now you have nothing but this job until you're twenty-five." During the 1960s, many trainees began their service at the Menlo Park store. "You would go from assistant buyer to merchandise manager and back to buyer," says Laba. "You were back and forth between the buying line and the selling line. You became knowledgeable of all facets of the building." R.H. Macy & Co., Bamberger's parent company, called its Executive Training Squad "the first organized retail program for the training of executives."

"Careers in the department store business are particularly attractive to young men and women who like a dynamic enterprise serving a growing population which seeks an ever higher standard of living," the company stated in 1963. "The people who worked at Bamberger's almost seemed like they belonged to a cult," states Laba. "[The employees] liked the company, the store and the atmosphere. It was not just a place to work." As the New York corporate office took notice of Bamberger's growth and success, executives and coworkers at the Macy's New York division grew jealous. Macy's corporate office cited Bamberger's for its "merchandising vigor" and "enriching the spirit of the communities in which it has stores."[80] Marvin Laba observes, "Macy's [New York] looked down at us. They were the mighty Macy's, and they had the bigger profile. [As Bamberger's became the most profitable and progressive arm of the corporation,] who wanted to be a Macy when we were Bamberger's? We were Bamberger's, and we did better."

As David Yunich had predicted, Bamberger's future was in the suburbs. Its direction and image were not dictated by a large downtown store. Department stores such as Marshall Field in Chicago and John Wanamaker in Philadelphia focused energy on their ornate emporiums and viewed their suburban stores as branches. Though it maintained its downtown Newark store, home of the corporate offices, and operated smaller urban branches in Morristown and Plainfield, Bamberger's embraced the economic and social benefits of the new breed of shopping centers. A 1961 *New York Times* article stated, "[Today's] practice is for families to pile into the car after supper and drive to the shopping center. Here the group often disperses—the wife to

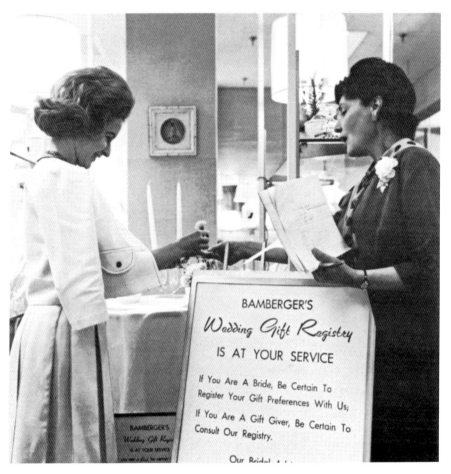

A shopper receives consultation from a bridal registry clerk at one of its suburban stores. This image dates from 1962. *Collection of the author.*

her shopping, the husband to his, and the youngsters to take in the sights…. The sense of an excursion is heightened by recorded music, attractive plantings of flowers and shrubs on the malls, and benches where shoppers can rest or chat. Informal attires contribute to the feeling."[81] Bamberger's thrived in northern New Jersey. In the early 1960s, Bamberger's enlarged the Menlo Park and Monmouth shopping centers in order to keep up with increased consumer demand in their growing communities. Its large Garden State Plaza location in Paramus was joined by a Gimbels branch, which further strengthened the shopping center's profile. Macy's New York division did not achieve the same suburban results as Bamberger's, especially with undersized stores that showed stagnant growth. "The New York stores

BAMBERGER'S EXCLUSIVE BRAND
SUPER-SOFT QUALITY TISSUES
AT EXCEPTIONALLY LOW PRICES

(A11) **Toilet tissue** in seven dainty pastels: peach, blue, canary, green, lilac, pink or aqua. Also all white. So soft, it rivals the finest facial tissues. Comes in storage carton. 100 rolls, **only 14.99**

18 rolls
ONLY 2.79

(B11) **Facial tissue.** Luxuriously soft cleansing tissues, fine enough for baby's tender skin. Peach, canary, blue, green, pink, lilac or aqua, or all white. Stock up now. 48 boxes, **only 10.99**

6 boxes
ONLY 1.39

EXCLUSIVE BRAND

Detecto bathroom scale
(C11) Watch your weight with this famous scale. Has patented mechanism for accuracy, even on thick carpets. Stainproof mat. Handle. Black, white, pink, **only 4.88**

Sturdy bathroom stool
(D11) Solid, one-piece plastic top and sturdy, chrome-plated legs will give years of rugged service. Lustrous finish wipes clean. White, black, pink, **only 8.44**

Pearlwick clothes hamper
(E11) Decorative diamond-glitter style, vinyl covered. Has gold-toned trim and towel ring. Generous size, for family use. White, black, pink, **only 9.97**

Pearlwick 3-piece ensemble only 13.44
(F11) Satin-stripe vinyl family size hamper with gold tone trim and towel ring, waste basket, tissue dispenser. White, pink, black.

Vinyl covered toilet seat
(G11) Smooth, sturdy, molded composition seat covered in jewel-tone vinyl with pearlized look in white, pink or black. Polyethylene hinges won't rust, corrode, **only 5.77**

Newark, Paramus, Menlo Park, Monmouth and Cherry Hill.

19

Even though Macy's sold its "Macy's Own Make" brand products in its namesake stores, Bamberger's also carried exclusive store brand housewares products. These branded products were largely discontinued by the late 1960s. *Collection of the author.*

never got the kind of attention like the Paramuses of the world," says Laba. "[Bamberger's] had it going a little earlier in life."

Located seventy-five miles southwest of Newark and just four miles west of Camden, the new Cherry Hill Mall was conceived to be the largest enclosed shopping mall south of New York. Designed by famed architect Victor Gruen and developed by James W. Rouse, the new Cherry Hill Mall was "something new in the way of shopping—more than a shopping center, a new community." The Philadelphia-based Strawbridge & Clothier department store was guaranteed the largest anchor building in the mall in Delaware Township, New Jersey. Additionally, Strawbridge & Clothier was given the right to choose a second anchor store. The business had historically battled for department store dominance in the Philadelphia market, so it avoided other Philadelphia stores when selecting this second anchor. Bamberger's was the perfect choice—lesser known than Strawbridge's but acclaimed for its "merchandising strength and good repute in New Jersey." The first phase of the Cherry Hill Mall opened on October 11, 1961. Strawbridge & Clothier reported, "The harmony of the spacious mall, high-ceilinged and lined with tropical trees, made it hard to believe that this was not a public garden....The new mall was a 'downtown' out in the country, a center of interest and liveliness, and a source of neighborhood pride."[82]

Bamberger's opened its 215,000-square-foot Cherry Hill store, its lone entry in the Philadelphia/South Jersey market, on September 21, 1962. The opening ceremonies were held in the "Court of Islands," a tropical garden filled with plants, bridges and 5-foot waterfalls. Miss New Jersey, Cherry Hill's own Georgia Malick, was a hostess of the event. Store manager Ray Gutter said, "Miss Malick, who began her climb toward the state beauty title as 'Miss Cherry Hill,' symbolized the warmth and charm we hope will characterize our relations with the local citizenry."[83] Bamberger's offered shopping options to the South Jersey market and for customers who traveled from Pennsylvania and beyond to see the revolutionary enclosed shopping complex. The Bamberger name was new to many customers yet was very familiar to transplanted residents from northern New Jersey. Bamberger's Cherry Hill very prominently added the tagline, "A division of R.H. Macy & Co." to advertising and building signage. This helped give the department store's name some validity. Back in Newark, president Herb Seegal and vice-president Ed Finkelstein were not impressed with Cherry Hill's initial sales figures. The Cherry Hill Mall was extremely popular, but both executives called it "large and unproductive" and felt it was not living up to its potential.[84] Seegal and Finkelstein invigorated the store's interior displays,

When it entered the southern New Jersey market in 1962, Bamberger's initially labeled the new store as "Cherry Hill–Camden" in its corporate materials. *Collection of the author.*

improved inventory levels and gave store management more autonomy from the Newark headquarters. The plan worked, and within a few years, Cherry Hill became one of Bamberger's top performing units. "Cherry Hill gave us an opportunity to learn about moving into other markets," says Borneo. "Bamberger's wasn't afraid to take risks."

After Cherry Hill, Bamberger's continued with expansion plans throughout the Garden State. In 1962, the department store purchased two tracts of land for future development plans: one in the Essex County community of Livingston and the other in Passaic County's Wayne Township. The company envisioned future stores in large enclosed regional centers, but both projects were many years from completion. In December 1963, Bamberger's agreed to anchor a new downtown shopping mall in Trenton. Located at Broad and Front Streets, the 200,000-square-foot store was part of a $15 million urban renewal project that included a relocated downtown Lit Brothers department store. Lit Brothers had threatened to leave downtown Trenton for many years due to its undersized and antiquated Broad Street store. Initially named the John Fitch Plaza, the center's plans were chronically stalled as residents fought the city over tax subsidies and parking concerns.[85] Bamberger's grew tired of the obstacles and withdrew from the project in 1965. "Trenton is not the easiest place to do business," states Handler. "It's old, political and doesn't have a high-end customer base." Lit Brothers also grew tired of the mall's construction delays. After voicing numerous complaints, Lits suddenly closed its old downtown Trenton store on May 31, 1968, and abandoned the city. At the end of 1969, plans for the John Fitch shopping complex, now named the Trenton Mall, were formally discarded.

Bamberger's was keenly aware of the challenges and changes in downtown Newark but remained committed to its downtown store and corporate headquarters. As suburban shopping became more convenient and competitive during the 1960s, many American department stores held special exhibitions at their downtown flagship locations, enticing former customers to return, even for a visit. From John Wanamaker in Philadelphia to Hutzler's in Baltimore and Filene's in Boston, department stores frequently held store-wide promotions that focused on a foreign country's culture and merchandise. In 1959, Bamberger's featured a Christmas exhibition of Swiss art and culture, followed by English art and culture in 1960. Christmas Across America was presented in 1961, and holiday festivals devoted to the Italian and Spanish Renaissance continued yearly. One letter from a customer to Bamberger's management read, "Bamberger's Christmas presentations contain ingredients of effort and risk and investment no other merchants in the land have been willing to undertake." One of the most elaborate events was the 1964 Renaissance Christmas III program, located on the fifth floor. Renaissance Christmas III was billed as "the most remarkable collection of priceless Renaissance treasure ever brought before America's people" and featured a royal coach of

A February 1962 newspaper advertisement proudly promotes the downtown Newark store with its nine selling floors, two hundred departments and two-level basement store. By the early 1960s, Bamberger's Newark store was steadily losing customers to suburban shoppers, even though over 2,600 parking spaces were available to shoppers who arrived by car. *Collection of the author.*

King Charles IV, tapestries and armor from Madrid, graphic prints by Picasso, Italian sculpture by Ubaldo Stiaccini and rare white peacocks from Portugal. Later years included a 1965 celebration of Marco Polo and an ambitious 1966 project that portrayed "the major forces influencing the history of Christmas." Bamberger's frequently received gold medal commendations from the National Retail Merchants Association for the best Christmas promotion in the United States.[86]

Special events at the Newark store were not confined to the Christmas season. Bamberger's presented classical concerts at Newark's Symphony Hall that featured Arthur Rubenstein, Leonard Bernstein and Leopold Stokowski. The department store also sponsored jazz appearances by Ella Fitzgerald, Sammy Davis Jr. and many others. One unusual presentation displayed the

A 1964 advertisement reinforced the toy department as an important component to Bamberger's business. The Newark's store's fourth-floor Bambergerland of Toys featured visits by Santa Claus and live snow-white Portuguese peacocks. *Collection of the author.*

resiliency of girdles with the store dressing a four-ton elephant in the world's largest foundation. The department store even surprised customers with Jerry Lewis working sales registers and Bob Hope modeling clothes. Christmas events were also celebrated at the suburban stores, but they were meant to generate excitement and ultimately bring customers back to Newark. The company operated Bampark parking lots and a drive-in auto center on Raymond Boulevard to accommodate customers arriving by automobile. The Newark basement store was still an attraction in itself, with its incredible bargains and unique merchandise. Bamberger's Newark was an imperfect business in an imperfect city. Bamberger's did a larger volume of business than any department store in the state and claimed more than half of the department store sales in Newark. But even as its stores were taking the New Jersey suburbs by storm, Newark was still its home base.

Newark's downtown continually evolved during the 1960s. City officials cited the city's former glory days, and supporters remained optimistic for its future. In 1966, the *Newark Evening News* ran an article that read, "Leisurely Shopping Gone, but Stores Still Thrive." The newspaper article

84

A female shopper examines one of the many pieces of art displayed throughout the Newark store during Christmas 1964. The display was a part of Renaissance Christmas III, a storewide event that brought suburban customers back to the Newark flagship during the holiday selling season. *Collection of the author.*

Left: The cover of this 1963 catalogue sums up Bamberger's role in New Jersey as a number one destination for housewares and home delivery options. The company's Teleservice department had operators based specifically out of its Newark, Plainfield and Cherry Hill stores. *Collection of the author.*

Right: Bamberger's promoted color television sets in this 1964 sales supplement. Department stores once served as the leading source for appliances and electronics before specialty retailers expanded their selections and offered more competitive pricing. *Collection of the author.*

acknowledged economic and social trends that were indicative of the decade. "Shopping in downtown Newark was more leisurely in days gone by.... Downtown Newark was THE place to shop. Weekend crowds flooded the city as housewives led their children through the stores. But with the advent of automobiles and increased population, shopping in Newark became a major headache."[87] But the article also praised the stores for adapting their merchandise to reflect the needs of downtown Newark shoppers and noted that the city's stores still carried "probably every [modern] thing for home and family."

Former Newark mayor Kenneth A. Gibson stresses another major social issue that ultimately affected Newark's public image. In most American cities, department stores rarely welcomed black customers, and many large stores expected black customers to limit their purchases to their basement stores. Gibson was the first African American mayor

The addition of Ohrbach's to Paramus's Bergen Mall helped set the center apart from its neighbor, the Garden State Plaza. Crowds filled the popular New York department store when it opened in August 1967. *Courtesy of the Newark Public Library.*

of a large American city. He states, "[Newark's] stores were not very open to everybody, like most of society in those days. They hired African Americans at menial jobs. If they were well dressed and well spoken, they could become an elevator operator." Depending on the level of merchandise and customer base, some stores were more "open" than others. Gibson continues, "Ohrbach's was easily established [in the African American] community. Bamberger's was pretty good, better than Hahne's, who had a snooty approach." After it received pressure from the newly formed Newark Business Industrial Coordinating Council, Bamberger's hired its first black sales clerks in late 1963. In early 1964, Bamberger's became the first American department store to integrate its display windows with "Negro manikins." The company stated, "The move [to integrate its displays] was made in consideration of the store's Negro customers and in the interest of realism."[88] Former resident Jeanette Thomas agrees that Bamberger's was more progressive

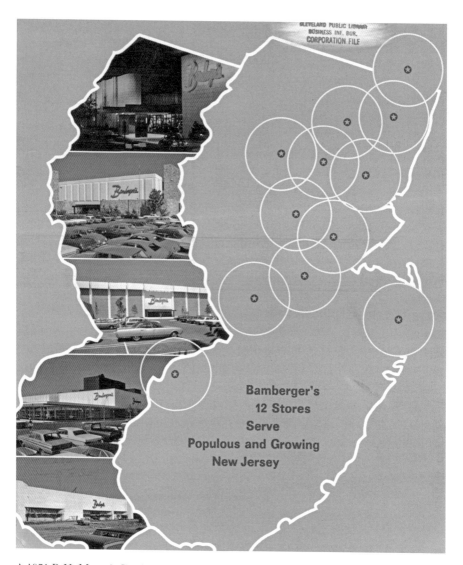

A 1971 R.H. Macy & Co. Annual Report celebrated the success of Bamberger's twelve locations. Bamberger's branches pictured (from top to bottom) are Nanuet, Willowbrook, East Brunswick, Menlo Park and Livingston. *Collection of the author.*

than its competitors. "[As an African American,] you couldn't even go in the back door at Hahne's." As the decade moved on, tensions grew in Newark, as well as in many American cities. By 1960, two-thirds of the city's population was black, but most of the schoolteachers were white. Black residents in the city's downtown Central Ward were charged high rents for deteriorating housing. As the city's newspapers touted the rebirth of Newark and its skyscraper construction, very few blacks were hired for those building projects.

In his book *Newark*, author John T. Cunningham states, "Newark was a city waiting for an explosion as it reached its anniversary year in 1966.... [Newark's government and business] leaders ignored the class discriminations and deepening poverty, preferring to believe that a celebration of 300 years of existence would help insure loyalty to Newark among the poor."[89] On May 18, 1966, with a parade that featured bands and flags, the city celebrated its industrial past, even though 50 percent of the city's residents were living well below poverty.

Chapter 7

"Newark Was Sick"

In April 1967, Reverend Martin Luther King Jr. predicted that at least ten American cities could erupt into "racial violence" that summer. King referred to these cities as "powder kegs" and noted, "The nation has not done anything to improve conditions in these areas." Dr. King urged a nonviolent approach to any demonstrations but added, "I'm afraid [my advice] will fall on deaf ears."[90] King expected Oakland, Washington, Chicago and Newark to experience turmoil. He apologized for his prediction but stated that intolerable conditions in these cities could not continue. The following month, the primarily white Newark city government officials sparred openly with black leaders and citizens over the appointment of a white secretary to the Board of Education and the planned demolition of several blocks of Central Ward housing for the construction of a medical and dental school. As the city's black community held public demonstrations throughout the downtown business district and infiltrated public meetings, Newark became the "powder keg" that Reverend King had described.

Relations between police and Newark's black community were tense. On July 12, 1967, John W. Smith, a black taxicab driver, was arrested for traffic violations. Rumors flew throughout Newark that Smith was clubbed and "stomped to death by police," and the incident sparked rioting that lasted five days. The "open rebellion," as termed by then-governor Richard J. Hughes, spread throughout the Central Ward and into the city's downtown.[91] By the time the situation stabilized, the immediate damage totaled $15 million, 1,300 arrests and twenty-six casualties. The 1967 Newark riot was the

In the mid-1950s, downtown Newark officials established Newark Sale Days, a promotion designed to bring shoppers back downtown. This advertisement states, "You know you'll find it in Newark, you're sure to find it at Bamberger's." *Collection of the author.*

country's second largest riot, after Los Angeles's Watts community had erupted in 1965.

Newark was irrevocably damaged in the public eye. Media based in New York City had easy access to capture footage of the rioting. As reports showed sniper fire and Molotov cocktails alongside massive looting and National Guard troops, Newark became "America's Most Dangerous City." Newark was called "an ugly city beset by slums and overcrowded housing" with a "soaring crime rate."[92] It was a damaging blow to a city in pain from decades of discriminatory practices and conditions. It was also a devastating hit to the city's commercial district. Early news reports stated that rioters were "determined to break out of the ghetto and sack the big center-city department stores like Bamberger's."[93] Area resident Ken Allan recalls, "During the riots, the rumor was that Bamberger's was broken into and looted and robbed." In reality, "the store was not directly hit," recalls former buyer Jeanette Thomas, "but around lunchtime, some black youths broke some windows, and we were told to go home." Although downtown department stores suffered some minimal damage, most of the destruction crippled the smaller stores that serviced the Central Ward, including areas along Springfield Avenue. Some of Newark's large downtown retailers tried to remain open during the disturbances but eventually closed until further notice. After opening for one half hour on July 14, S. Klein received "vile phone calls threatening us with all kinds of damage" and closed the Broad Street store soon after.[94] Mark S. Handler was Bamberger's president in July 1967 and remembered, "The riots were an awful period of time. The store didn't sustain damage, but we were closed for about three days. There were police and National Guard [all around the store]. The police were very heavy-handed. It was a very stressful time." When the demonstrations subsided and Bamberger's reopened, "no throngs

On July 15, 1967, National Guard troops were stationed throughout downtown Newark as a result of the Springfield Avenue racial disturbances. This armed tank is parked outside the Bamberger's Auto Center on Raymond Boulevard, only two blocks from the main downtown store. *Courtesy of the Newark Public Library.*

of shoppers milled in the [downtown] department stores."[95] Newark's daytime population stayed away from their offices and the retail district for weeks. The city was left with a deserted downtown and an angry and divided community.

Newark was not the only New Jersey city that experienced unrest in July 1967. Plainfield, home to Bamberger's second suburban store, was also plagued with violence. Tensions between Plainfield's growing black community and police and city government officials led to several days of rioting and shootings, resulting in the death of a city police officer. The Plainfield disturbance was viewed as a "spillover from the Newark disorders," and city officials were cited for neglecting Plainfield's "growing disadvantaged population."[96] Looting and violent confrontations centered in downtown Plainfield. Although Bamberger's Plainfield store was located a few blocks from the city center, the store suffered sales losses and a permanently torn community. "Plainfield took a huge hit after the riots, and there was a tremendous amount of white flight," recalls former resident Rosemary

Friedrich. The Plainfield riots damaged multiple properties in the city's West End, home to a sizable black middle-class community, but left some "upper crust" white neighborhoods, such as Sleepy Hollow, untouched. "After the riots, people couldn't give their homes away in Plainfield," states resident Gary Boni. The Plainfield Bamberger's remained open during the periods of unrest and continued its role as one of the city's economic engines. "Bamberger's still brought so many people back into town after the riots," says local historian Nancy Piwowar.

After the April 1968 assassination of Reverend Martin Luther King Jr., rioting returned to Newark. Even as city officials and community leaders asked for calm in the city's streets, hundreds of fires blazed and dozens of businesses were looted and destroyed. Although the destruction was not comparable in scale to the riots of 1967, the unrest further damaged Newark's image and proved that the city was unstable. Random public demonstrations occurred in subsequent years, and businesses and middle-class residents fled the city. By the end of the 1960s, Newark reportedly had "one of the unhealthiest populations in America."[97] "Broad and Market Streets once were the nerve center [of Newark] and crossed to form one of the busiest intersections in the nation," read an Associated Press report. "[As of the late 1960s,] most of the stores, Bamberger's, Ohrbach's, Klein's and others, are still in the area. But Broad and Market Streets are now filled with pimps, winos, pushers, and guys selling hot watches."[98]

"Newark was sick, but the rest of the [Bamberger's] business was enormously healthy," recalls then-president Mark S. Handler. Company reports from R.H. Macy & Co. made little to no mention of Newark's climate and any impact to the Bamberger's downtown store and headquarters. "The continued addition of productive and profitable suburban stores is the key to Bamberger's future growth," stated an R.H. Macy & Co. corporate report. By the end of the 1960s, it was Macy's second largest division in size and its most profitable. Over the course of the decade, Bamberger's sales figures doubled as New Jersey's population constantly grew. On September 20, 1967, the long-awaited 265,000-square-foot Willowbrook store in Wayne opened its doors. Announced in October 1962, Willowbrook originally had anticipated a 1964 opening, but zoning issues and changing designs delayed its opening. Bamberger's was Willowbrook Mall's first tenant, and the rest of the center opened in phases. Once completed, Willowbrook Mall was the nation's largest enclosed shopping center. It was billed as a "new downtown," an intentional or unintentional reference to the once-mighty downtown Newark retail district.

Left: Bamberger's Willowbrook Mall store in Wayne, New Jersey, opened on September 20, 1967. The largest shopping center catered to an affluent and fast-growing market. Its primary trade area included Essex, Passaic and Morris Counties. *Collection of the author.*

Below: On October 16, 1969, Bamberger's opened its first and only New York store at the Nanuet Mall. located only about fifteen miles from Paramus, New Jersey. Bamberger's officials convinced the New York headquarters that the Nanuet Mall was an important center and was best operated by the Newark division. *Collection of the author.*

In 1968, Rockland County was New York's smallest county but also boasted New York's second fastest–growing population. Bulldozers reigned, as shopping centers, schools, apartments, offices and homes were rapidly constructed to accommodate the expanding community. As the county's development progressed, R.H. Macy & Co. expressed strong interest in a newly planned fifty-five-acre shopping center named Nanuet Mall. Although Bamberger's had never operated in New York and Macy's had never crossed the river into New Jersey, Bamberger's expressed interest in the site. "I wanted the Nanuet store," states then–Bamberger's president Mark S. Handler. "I felt that it folded easily into Bamberger's territory." Macy's formally stated that the New York division had enough stores of its own and turned the store over to Bamberger's. "The rapid growth [in Rockland County] is evident in the Bamberger's and Sears stores about to sprout in a huge plot in Nanuet, in the mobile homes hurriedly set up as bank branches, and in the boom-townish quality of many small shopping centers," reported the *New York Times*.[99] The 225,000-square-foot store opened on October 16, 1969. Nanuet was the only Bam's location that ever operated in New York State.

Left: Bamberger's chronicled the construction progress at East Brunswick throughout several issues of the company news magazine *Around the Clock. Courtesy of the Newark Public Library.*

Right: The September 1970 issue of *Around the Clock* profiled the grand opening of the new East Brunswick store. The stand-alone store opened on September 10, 1970. *Courtesy of the Newark Public Library.*

The employee magazine, *Around the Clock*, celebrated the 1970 opening of the East Brunswick Bamberger's. Singer Julius La Rosa and cartoonist Kay Kato were on hand for the opening festivities. *Collection of the author.*

As the 1960s came to a close, Bamberger's announced further expansions into central New Jersey. Bamberger's officials met with various Lawrence Township committees and community groups in November 1968 and discussed plans for a new $20 million enclosed shopping mall. Bamberger's identified itself as the mall's developer, and rumors circulated that Ohrbach's, Abraham and Straus, and Sears would join Bamberger's at the Lawrence Township mall located at the intersection of Route 1 and Quaker Bridge Road, halfway between Trenton and Princeton. Mall developers anticipated a 1971 opening, but the center's debut was many more years in the future. Bamberger's eleventh store opened on September 10, 1970, in East Brunswick, New Jersey. The 244,000-square-foot department store, located about seven miles southeast of the Rutgers University New Brunswick campus, was a single location that was later joined by JCPenney and a small enclosed shopping complex. One former employee describes the East Brunswick store as "a stand alone store in a nothing mall." It catered to a more moderate customer than some of the other Bamberger's locations. "Whatever didn't sell in Menlo Park was shipped to East Brunswick," states the employee.

In 1970, New Jersey was the most densely populated state in the country. A 1971 corporate report stated, "The Census Bureau has projected a 25% increase in New Jersey's population in the next decade, which will give Bamberger's a dynamic growth market for its present and future stores." Former executive Rudolph Borneo says, "There was a real sense of concern with downtown [Newark]. There was an immediate customer drop-off after the riots. But because it was the store where the executives had been [located and trained], the company wanted to keep focused on the city [and keep the store open]." As residents and shoppers fled the city, Bamberger's future was clearly in the New Jersey suburbs, with large stores that appealed to the state's continually growing middle-class demographic.

Chapter 8

Aftermath

Throughout the early part of the 1960s, Bamberger's adopted many slogans that promoted the viability and integrity of the massive Newark flagship store. Advertisement bylines stated, "You Know You'll Find It in Newark—You're Sure to Find It at Bamberger's," "You Accomplish a Lot at Bamberger's Newark," "The Best Comes from Bamberger's" and "Newark Is Newer." These accompanied Bamberger's standard slogan: "New Jersey's Greatest Store—One of America's Finest." However, after the July 1967 riots, the department store quickly and simply changed its catchphrase to "Bamberger's—New Jersey." Store president Herbert Seegal told the *Newark Evening News*, "It is too early to predict the impacts of the riots on retail business in the city."[100] Seegal claimed that there would be a "period of adjustment" and that "it will take some time to reestablish a retail climate here." The "period of adjustment" included the closure of Chase Department Store, formerly Kresge-Newark. Chase Department Store was hemorrhaging money, and by November 1967, owner David Chase was searching for a new owner for his business. In December, Chase leased the store to the mass merchandiser Two Guys. At the final clearance sale, shoppers, "like bees over a honeycomb," descended into the store known for its elegant hand-carved columns and Tiffany lamps. An elevator operator bemoaned, "I feel so bad. It would have been 25 years in June. I wanted so very much to have my anniversary watch. I would have been so proud of it. It's just a small thing but it would have meant so much to me."[101] On

In 1969, Bamberger's opened the Pacesetter Shop in its downtown Newark flagship store. The Pacesetter Shop was "the setting for the presentation of tomorrow's fashion look." The department was an example of Bamberger's commitment to innovative displays and updated interior features. *Collection of the author.*

February 11, 1968, Chase closed its doors and ended the legacy of its predecessor, Kresge. On September 6, 1968, Two Guys opened in the first three floors and basement of the former Chase store. Two Guys president Frederick Zissu predicted that the new store would "play an important part in revitalizing downtown shopping" and expressed "faith in Newark's future as a major shopping area and as an economic and residential center."[102] Two Guys' entry into downtown Newark kept retail transactions alive in the landmark Broad Street building. But the loss of Chase Department Store meant one less option for the middle-class customer who also shopped at Bamberger's and Hahne's.

Downtown businesses worked hard to improve Newark's reputation. The First National State Bank of New Jersey placed a full-page advertisement in the *Newark Evening News* after the riots: "In the past decade, Newark has been moving forward as rapidly as any other city in the United States. We recognize that there exist serious problems, among them the inescapable fact that Newark is the only city in the country whose daytime population doubles each working day. The people of Newark, including the business community, have been working toward solutions. They will continue to do so." The bank cited many "good things" that had recently occurred in the city. Newark had built "more low income housing per capita than any city in the United States," housed the city's great "skilled and unskilled" labor market and was home to the growing Newark Airport, Port Newark and many new "major and fully occupied" office buildings. "These are just a few of the reasons why Newark is a growing city and will continue to grow," stated the bank. "The tragedy of recent days is behind us. Now is the time for everyone who lives and works in Newark to get on with the business of building this city in peace and understanding." It was an optimistic statement but a tall order. Regular demonstrations and future disturbances challenged that optimism.

The once mighty flagship Bamberger's was permanently crippled after the 1967 riots. Its "Third Floor Boulevard of Fashion" was no longer a popular destination for middle-class customers. The 1.2-million-square-foot building perpetually closed off floor space as it adapted to declining sales and fewer customers. Buyer Jeanette Thomas felt "the best thing at Bamberger's was the meat department." The meat department was a lower-level fixture, but by 1972, it and "everything except for the [budget] clothing was basically removed from the basement store," says Thomas. "Newark became a value-oriented store," says former executive Rudolph Borneo. "The customer was always looking for bargains. It didn't offer any 'day-in, day-out' growth." "After the riots, [Newark] had totally changed," says Morristown employee Larry Davis. "It was like a war zone, but we ended up going to [the downtown Newark shopping district] for urban wear." As its once loyal white customer base fled downtown, employee Ken Allan recalls that Bamberger's attempted a major outreach to the African American community. "I once worked in a department called the Main Man Shop. It was on the first floor, and they took out a couple of display windows [in order to fit it onto the sales floor]. It was very cutting edge, stylized and pretty wild. [Bamberger's Newark]

FASHION FOOTNOTES

THE BLACK LOOK

"Black is beautiful" is a rallying cry for pride in heritage. Many of today's modern black girls with self-knowledge and all the inner qualities that make for individuality—dress reflecting this.

The look is African with a long straight hanging Bubus dress of large clashing prints and designs. The cut also can resemble a long Empire waisted peasant dress. The animal look with bold stripes, spots or fur patterns is popular. With the black look, most of the body should be covered with only the ankles, hands, lower arms, face and neck exposed. The cloth Gaylay, or turban headwrap, usually matches the dress and completes the ensemble.

Jewelry is a must and the more the better. Large dangling earrings, lots of bracelets, rings and long necklaces can add flair. But remember, choose only ornaments reflecting black heritage. Bags should be soft and of the shoulder carrying variety, preferably made from cloth. They too can be large prints or even the same pattern as the dress. Leather or suede with fringe is not the look.

Sandals or thongs are a must for footwear and of course never wear heel shoes or boots. Makeup should be so natural that you have to look twice to see it. Natural is the word too in hairstyles with the Afro a must.

Dashiki* tops are made from printed material and come in colorful designs to match any temperament. They're worn over pants by men and by women in longer lengths.

Our own Bamberger's model is Corinne Smith who enjoys wearing the Black Look to work. Also a talented seamstress, Corinne made these clothes from material purchased in Bamberger's Fabric Department.

also spelled Dansaiki and in Swahili it is spelled Danshekie

"Black Is Beautiful" was the theme of a November 1970 Bamberger's promotion. After the late 1960s, Bamberger's gave greater attention to its African American shoppers and inner-city customers. The "Black Is Beautiful" promotion was called "a rallying cry for pride in heritage." *Courtesy of the Newark Public Library.*

wanted to make African American shoppers feel that it was their store. But even the middle-income black customers were avoiding the downtown area like the plague." Allan remembers a large 1974 event at the Newark store: "They held performances of the musical *Raisin* downtown, and Bamberger's went all out to promote it. They even installed a special box office in the corner display window." But Allan considers this the Newark store's last big promotion as a flagship store. Bamberger's transitioned its massive building from a department store that catered to all income levels to a downsized retail operation that housed the company's popular Teleservice phone order department and corporate headquarters. The growing business continually needed more room for offices that supported the department store's extremely successful and profitable suburban operations.

Bamberger's opened its much-anticipated Livingston store on October 5, 1971. Originally announced back in 1964, the 219,000-square-foot store was located just thirteen miles from downtown Newark. The Livingston Bamberger's was also only five miles from the Mall at Short Hills, home of some of New York's finest stores such as B. Altman & Co., Bonwit Teller and Bloomingdale's. Bamberger's had studied a possible entry into Short Hills but ultimately concentrated its expansion on Livingston. "[Bamberger's] not going into Short Hills might have been a miss, but our Livingston store was not that far away," says Borneo. Livingston was Bamberger's twelfth department store location, and it opened in grand style. Actress Eileen Fulton and disc jockey Julius La Rosa made special appearances, and more than three hundred children, ages seven and under, cast their handprints in cement under the store's flagpole. A plaque under the flagpole read, "This space belongs forever to the children whose hands are immortalized here. Bamberger's will always remember the day we met."[103] The architectural design of the Livingston store was more contemporary than recently opened stores. "I always felt that the Livingston store seemed associated more with Macy's than Bamberger's," says Morristown employee Larry Davis. In 1972, Bamberger's attached its store to the new Livingston Mall. Livingston Mall featured Sears, Bamberger's Morristown rival M. Epstein and Newark's Hahne's. It was Hahne's first foray into a New Jersey shopping center.

Bamberger's Cherry Hill Mall store was the company's only store in the South Jersey and Philadelphia market. After its 1962 opening, the company tested different merchandise formats and offerings as it figured out the area customers' tastes. Philadelphia-area customers were more conservative and value conscious than those in the New York/northern New Jersey market

Left: The November 1971 *Around the Clock* magazine proudly covered the opening of the Livingston store. Livingston became one of the company's most important branch stores and further usurped the Newark store's customer base. *Courtesy of the Newark Public Library.*

Below: Livingston Mall opened in 1972 with Bamberger's, Hahne's and M. Epstein as the mall anchor stores. The Livingston Mall Bamberger's store opened almost six months before the rest of the center. *Courtesy of the Newark Public Library.*

Hahne's first shopping center branch store was located at the Livingston Mall. Opened in 1972, Hahne's expanded the store over the next several years, and by 1981, the Livingston Mall Hahne's unofficially became the company flagship store in terms of quality and depth of merchandise. *Courtesy of the Newark Public Library.*

but demanded quality and style. By the early 1970s, Bamberger's outpaced sales figures at Strawbridge & Clothier, its Cherry Hill Mall rival and developer of the groundbreaking shopping center. Bamberger's formula—giving local authority to each store's management team—was a recipe for success. An R.H. Macy & Co. 1973 corporate statement said that there were "preliminary commitments for two additional stores in central and northern New Jersey and for another two in the Philadelphia suburban area." On August 9, 1973, Bamberger's opened its first Pennsylvania store at the new Oxford Valley Mall in Langhorne. Philadelphia department store stalwarts John Wanamaker and Gimbels, along with JCPenney and about 130 stores, joined Bamberger's. The Oxford Valley Bamberger's offered many different services along with its standard full complement of merchandise. A large budget store, the 106-seat Carriage House restaurant, a snack bar, a travel agency and a beauty salon were among its many features. After a successful opening in Oxford Valley, Bamberger's moved deeper into the Philadelphia market. In 1974, a branch opened at the Springfield Mall in Delaware County, followed by a second South

Jersey location at the Deptford Mall. Bamberger's Deptford Mall opened in August 1975 and competed directly with John Wanamaker. "When [Bamberger's] went into the Philadelphia market, John Wanamaker and Strawbridge & Clothier were both withered and not well run," recalls former president Mark Handler. "We came in with a fresh look and paid attention to each store."

In 1973, downtown Newark continued to decline. Many retailers, including Bamberger's, Hahne's and Two Guys, reduced their hours due to sluggish sales and nighttime safety concerns. In June, S. Klein on Broad Street reduced its sales space by half. Klein's management stated that the consolidation would help give closer control between the customers and merchandise and that "suburban stores proved that you don't need multi floors" to successfully operate a department store. S. Klein president Robert Maddux stressed, "Klein's is confident of the future of downtown Newark and has no plans to leave the city."[104] The situation was different at Ohrbach's on Market Street. Located in the former Bamberger's store at Market and Halsey Streets, Ohrbach's decided to close its downtown Newark location after the Christmas 1973 season. Company officials reported, "Business [at the Newark store] has been declining over a decade and in the past few years the deterioration in sales has accelerated." The January 31, 1974 closing was a blow to downtown Newark's image as a retail destination. Bamberger's, Ohrbach's immediate neighbor, released a message: "[Bamberger's] would like to assure you personally that we have no intention whatsoever of closing its Newark store."[105] "Market Street became pretty rough after Ohrbach's closed," recalls former resident and Bamberger's employee Ken Allan. Newark was dealt a harsh second blow in June 1975 when all remaining S. Klein locations ceased operations. A victim of its parent company, McCrory Stores Corporation, S. Klein's closure gave customers one less reason to come downtown.

By the mid-1970s, Paramus had transformed from rich farmland into a congested suburban commercial area located in the nation's tenth wealthiest county. Four large shopping centers lined the town's retail corridors, and residents demanded that the local government halt further development. Residents complained that Paramus had become nothing more than "gerry-built roadside retail stores, many of which are little more than cement-block warehouses encased in plastic and lighted by neon," along with "miles of highway-sign blight and retail honky-tonk with unbelievable traffic congestion."[106] Even though Paramus's department stores paid enough of the borough's property taxes to take care of its municipal services, the

By the 1970s, Paramus was home to four major shopping malls: the Garden State Plaza, the Bergen Mall, the Fashion Center at Paramus and the Paramus Park Mall. Riverside Square Mall in nearby Hackensack added to the retail density. The Fashion Center included Fifth Avenue retailers B. Altman, Lord & Taylor and Best & Co. However, Best & Co. stores liquidated in late 1970, shortly before the Paramus store opened. *Courtesy of the Newark Public Library.*

town council elected to curb retail construction and focus on light industrial complexes and office buildings as future projects.

Back in May 1957, Bamberger's became the first retailer to make its mark in Paramus at its Garden State Plaza store. Bergen Mall opened just months after Garden State Plaza, and the two developments enjoyed a healthy competition, although Bamberger's always outpaced the sales figures at Bergen Mall's Stern's department store. When Gimbels joined Bamberger's in 1960, it gave the Garden State Plaza a competitive advantage over Bergen Mall. In August 1967, just one month after rioting broke out in downtown Newark, Ohrbach's opened a second New Jersey branch at the Bergen Mall. Ohrbach's advertised "high fashions at low prices," and thousands of local residents "burst into the new store" on opening day and "[ran] up the bright, new aisles to throng counters of specially priced merchandise."[107] Bergen Mall, perceived as "the grand old lady of Route 4," completed a $1.2 million roofing project in September 1973.[108] Mall officials optimistically felt that the steel and Plexiglass covering would modernize the sixteen-year-old center and address fierce retail competition and changing shopping patterns.

Although Garden State Plaza and Bergen Mall were located only three minutes apart, the two centers served different clienteles, for the most part. Garden State Plaza was closer to the Garden State Parkway exit ramps, and its massive Bamberger's store, along with northern New Jersey's only Gimbels branch, drew a regional customer base. Bergen Mall was slightly smaller and was situated closer to some of the community's residential neighborhoods. "Stern's [at Bergen Mall] was a quality store and a good competitor to Bamberger's," says local historian Bill Leaver. "The two stores were neck and neck, but Stern's, at least for us, became more convenient." In 1975, Garden State Plaza announced a $20 million expansion and facelift that "enabled the plaza to stay competitive with the covered shopping malls that have been built in the area in the last few years."[109] The expansion included 400,000 square feet added to the massive 1.35-million-square-foot shopping center. The Garden State Plaza Corporation, a separate entity within the R.H. Macy & Co. parent company, owned the center and spearheaded its expansion. However, zoning issues and design changes delayed the project's completion for almost a decade. This was not the company's first experience with enclosing an outdoor center. Back in December 1967, Edison's Menlo Park Shopping Center added a roof to the formerly open-air complex. The Menlo Park conversion included a 72,500-square-foot addition to the Bamberger's store, along with an indoor fountain, an aquarium and a circular memorial to Thomas Edison that featured colored lights and an exhibition stage. The Monmouth Shopping Center, home to a Bamberger's store, embarked on a $25 million expansion that included a roof for the outdoor center. However, the Garden State Plaza Bamberger's had the highest sales volume and profits of any Macy's branch store across the country. Modernization was critical to the center's continued success, and any improvements would enhance the store's already impressive sales figures.

As the Garden State Plaza and Bergen Mall neared completion in 1957, Paramus officials became concerned about anticipated traffic congestion. In addition to shoppers who traveled by automobile, Route 4 served as an important weekend travel route between New York City and the popular Catskill Mountain resorts. In February 1957, Paramus mayor Fred C. Galda proposed an ordinance that prohibited Sunday business except for "works of necessity and charity." The ordinance allowed for the sale of prepared food, milk, non-alcoholic beverages and newspapers only. Mayor Galda stated, "Paramus is a suburban community and the Council's primary

The Fashion Center at Paramus opened in 1967 and became the third-largest shopping center in Paramus. Eventually anchored by Lord & Taylor and B. Altman & Co., the Fashion Center acted as an upscale alternative to the Bergen Mall and Garden State Plaza. In 1974, Paramus Park Mall entered the crowded Paramus market, with Abraham and Straus and Sears. The four malls brought in more retail sales than any other zip code in the country. *Courtesy of the Newark Public Library.*

consideration is the achievement and maintenance of a satisfactory living environment for present and prospective inhabitants of the borough."[110] Bamberger's and other large retailers actively fought the ban until 1959, when the state legislature allowed communities to support Sunday closings by voter referendum. In 1960, by popular referendum, twelve counties endorsed the limited blue law, which prohibited Sunday sales of clothing, building and lumber supplies, appliances, furniture and furnishings. Sales of other retail goods that were deemed "necessities," such as gas, drugs and food, were permitted. The matter was taken to the New Jersey Supreme Court in April 1960. Bamberger's, discounter Two Guys and department store retailer Perth Amboy–based Reynolds Brothers were the plaintiffs in the case. The court upheld Sunday sales bans in the selected counties, including Bergen, and Sunday closings became part of Paramus's identity.

Chapter 9

Rags to Riches

As Bamberger's thrived in New Jersey's suburbs, Macy's New York division, with its massive and iconic Herald Square flagship and fifteen branch stores located mostly throughout Long Island and Westchester County, produced meager profits. Macy's New York stores offered a broad selection of everyday merchandise that failed to excite shoppers. It relied on its moniker as the "World's Biggest Store" and remained visible through its annual Thanksgiving Day Parade and Fourth of July fireworks presentations. By the 1960s, Macy's faced stiff competition from rival Bloomingdale's, which had transformed its store from a middle-of-the-road department store to a fashion leader on New York's Upper East Side. Corporate management decided to apply some of the successful tactics that had provided spectacular results at its Bamberger's and San Francisco divisions to Herald Square. The Bamberger's management team that had changed Bamberger's from an all-encompassing moderately priced retailer to one that offered large assortments of "most wanted goods," trendy designer labels and intriguing displays had included Edward S. Finkelstein, Herbert Seegal, Herbert Friedman and Philip Schlein.

"The rebuilding of the New York division was a huge job," states former company president Mark S. Handler. Finkelstein, then-president of Macy's San Francisco and the former vice-president of merchandising and sales promotion at Bamberger's, was transferred to Herald Square. Finkelstein had spearheaded The Cellar concept at the San Francisco division flagship store. The Cellar was "an attractive complex of departments selling housewares, gourmet food, and candy, with a bar room type of restaurant and contemporary fashion shops" located in the store's former bargain basement.[111] Inspired by London's Harrods, Finkelstein had introduced The Cellar to San Francisco Bay Area shoppers in 1973 and reinvented the store's image. In the fall of 1976, The Cellar debuted at Herald Square. The former bargain basement, described as "a [once] cavernous and rather ungainly sprawl of merchandise," generated publicity and greater sales at the dowdy store.[112] Macy's discontinued other low-producing departments on its upper floors and replaced that merchandise with fashion-forward clothing lines. "Ed [Finkelstein] started the thought process behind The Cellar when he ran the housewares department [in San Francisco]," says former executive Rudolph Borneo. "Ed made a big push and turned the stores into a fashion business, and this included the home merchandise." During the 1976 holiday season, Macy's New York, "long considered one of the giant sleeping bears of American retailing," produced the largest sales increases of any New York department store over the previous year.[113]

The situation was very different in Newark. "When you look at Newark, it's not San Francisco or Herald Square," states Borneo. "It just wasn't that kind of flagship store." The Newark store was maintained but downsized. Though many architectural designs and displays by famed commercial architect Raymond Loewy were featured in the building, the store had last been fully renovated in 1950. Bamberger's Newark store stood frozen in time, with its twenty-foot ceilings and ornate wooden detailing, amidst a decaying downtown retail district. "You could still see the signs of when it was a much more elegant place, but it was shopworn," recalls former buyer Ken Allan. "By the mid-1970s, the store started looking like a vault. It was easy to drive by and wonder if it was still open." Bamberger's leadership even contemplated a move to the Meadowlands district, near New Jersey's sports stadiums. "The divisional vice-president had sent memos listing the progress of the project, but it was shelved due to environmental concerns," recalls Allan. Bamberger's never relocated its Newark retail store and headquarters.

Back in 1959, Two Guys had spearheaded the effort to repeal Sunday blue law restrictions. The corporation was unsuccessful in its campaign. However, during the 1975 Christmas selling season, all Two Guys stores opened on Sundays, including those affected by blue law ordinances. Some counties limited the sales of certain items, but Two Guys ignored all restrictions. North Jersey communities cited Two Guys for violations for selling prohibited items. Prosecution of those summonses was put off. The rebellion escalated the following year. Bamberger's and Hahne's joined Two

Guys and opened their downtown stores for business on Sunday, November 28, in defiance of New Jersey's strict Sunday shopping bans. The Sunday openings were the first for Newark, and all three stores reported brisk sales. Many shoppers returned to downtown Newark and hoped to relive holiday memories of the past bustling district. "When [the downtown stores] opened on Sunday in 1976, a lot of people were crestfallen," recalls Allan. "They went down to Hahne's basement, and there was no Santa Claus or merry-go-round. It was just clearance merchandise." Hahne's downtown Newark store dropped its Santa Claus visits in 1974, and Bamberger's eliminated Santa in 1977.

Even though the Sunday openings were illegal, they were hugely successful for Newark in terms of sales. But Essex County officials issued summonses to all three department stores and stated that store personnel, from sales staff to management, would be subject to arrest. The summonses read, "Please be advised that the Essex County prosecutor's office cannot tolerate open and flagrant violations of state penal statutes."[114] The following week, Bamberger's, Hahne's and Two Guys defied the citations and opened additional stores. Bamberger's stores in Plainfield, Menlo Park, East Brunswick and Willowbrook challenged the ban. Municipalities issued hundreds of summonses, and four Two Guys' employees were arrested at the Watchung store. Two Guys, with the support and backing of Bamberger's, Hahne's and other large New Jersey retailers, took the matter to New Jersey Superior Court. On March 10, 1977, Superior Court judge Sylvia Pressler ruled that "the prohibitions were unconstitutionally arbitrary" and said "the Sunday closing law…cannot stand." However, in the Paramus area, the sale of "necessity" merchandise such as food, gasoline and drugs was allowed. These specific blue laws received strong community support. Judge Pressler agreed, reasoning that the Paramus ordinance "did not discriminate," in sharp contrast to other communities' restrictions that banned all sales, irrespectively.[115] Judge Pressler's decision remained under appeal until the New Jersey State Superior Court decided in November 1979 to uphold the decision and allow Sunday sales. Bamberger's stores in Menlo Park, Plainfield and Monmouth immediately embraced the court's decision. Sales were "very busy" in Menlo Park but "light to moderate" in Plainfield as residents adjusted to the new Sunday shopping option.[116]

In the mid-1970s, Bamberger's aggressively expanded past the metropolitan New York/North Jersey market. When R.H. Macy & Co. officials announced a replacement store in downtown White Plains, New York, Bamberger's wanted to run the operation. "They wanted to prove [to

the New York corporate management team] what a dominant store division Bamberger's was," recalls Allan. "But they lacked one thing: the name. Bamberger's forgot that [ultimately] they were just a division of R.H. Macy." The company opened five large locations from 1976 to 1977 throughout its traditional New Jersey and Philadelphia markets. Bamberger's had committed to these stores many years in advance of their openings, but inflation fears were not ignored by the corporate management team in Newark. During this period, department stores showed favorable sales trends despite the increase in the cost of living and rising unemployment figures. R.H. Macy & Co. reported in 1976, "Any resurgence in inflation will penalize disposable income and is likely to inhibit any sharp rebound in the housing and consumer durable sectors of the economy." But New Jersey's economy had fared better than that of other states across the country and supported growth.

A large Bamberger's opened as a new anchor store at the Quaker Bridge Mall in 1976. The mall was located midway between Trenton and Princeton. The new mall store added strain to the smaller Princeton Bamberger's. Officials decided to close the longtime Princeton store in 1980. *Collection of the author.*

On March 18, 1976, Bamberger's opened a 221,000-square-foot unit at the new Quaker Bridge Mall, located between Trenton and Princeton. Despite being located approximately four miles from the company's longtime Princeton store, R.H. Macy invested in a 50 percent ownership of the new shopping mall. Hahne's, Sears and JCPenney joined Bamberger's in the project. Although the center became successful and spurred area retail and residential growth, Quaker Bridge Mall got off to a tricky start. "Quaker Bridge was a strange mall," says Allan. "It was seen [by the locals] as part of the Philadelphia market. Hahne's struggled [at the mall]. Customers asked, 'Who are you?' But Hahne's employees did well opening new credit cards." Area shoppers were relatively familiar with the Bamberger name from its Princeton store, and the department store did not face the same issue as the new Quaker Bridge Hahne's. Undaunted by Hess's dominance,

Bamberger's entered the Allentown, Pennsylvania market as part of the new Lehigh Valley Mall. The 218,000-square-foot Lehigh Valley Mall store opened on September 2, 1976, and joined John Wanamaker and Sears as the mall anchors. Hess's, Allentown's famous promotional department store, remained committed to its downtown Hamilton Street landmark and elected not to enter Lehigh Valley Mall. Hess's ultimately regretted the decision in later years. Bamberger's continued down the New Jersey coast with a location at the Ocean County Mall in Toms River. The location was slightly smaller than recently constructed Bamberger stores and opened on March 10, 1977. The Ocean County Mall helped fill a retail void in New Jersey's growing shore communities. Just five months later, Bamberger's returned to North Jersey with a new store at the Rockaway Townsquare in Dover, New Jersey. The 260,000-square-foot store opened on August 11, 1977. Rockaway Townsquare served North Jersey's growing western communities but siphoned off shoppers from local downtowns such as Morristown, just twenty minutes from the new enclosed mall. "Rockaway pretty much decimated the Morristown store," says Allan. The Morristown Bamberger's, the company's first branch store, was also challenged by a major downtown construction that lasted through the mid-1980s. "The Headquarters Plaza complex was part of what caused downtown [Morristown's] demise," says Morristown historian Margaret Brady. "Urban renewal projects became corrupt, and many local low-income homes [near the construction site] were cleared, but it left a huge pit. There was a big hole in the ground for about ten years." Bamberger's Morristown store was located across the street from Headquarters Plaza, and small merchants near the department store were devastated by the construction delays. The newly built Interstate 287 ran through Morristown and cut the community in half, changing the town's small-town image. However, Bamberger's Morristown hung through the obstacles and remained a contributor to the company's sales and profit figures, albeit at proportionately lower levels.

By the end of the 1970s, the situation at the Newark headquarters building seemed as precarious as ever. "There was some civic pressure to the keep the Newark store open," says Handler. "But there was also self-imposed pressure because the store's real estate became worthless." In 1977, Bamberger's closed all exterior display windows and shut half of the store's outer entrances. The changes were meant to safeguard the building's storefront and reduce pilferage that occurred through the exit door traffic. By 1979, all evening hours were eliminated and store space continued to shrink. "Customers would come to the downtown store if they wanted

Bamberger's joined John Wanamaker and JCPenney at Allentown, Pennsylvania's Lehigh Valley Mall. The Lehigh Valley store opened in September 1976 and did not directly compete at the mall with Hess's, the area's popular hometown department store. *Collection of the author.*

some particular piece of merchandise because they had the stock in the back room," states Allan. "It also became known that the store wasn't that busy." Allan recalls working the sales floor during one Christmas season in the late 1970s. "[Bamberger's] would stay open until 9:00 p.m. during the holidays, and I remember working the book department on the sixth floor. One night, I had a customer at 6:00 p.m., and that was it. One of the reasons the store stayed open was because of the company's large corporate headquarters [located on the building's upper floors]. There was a saying that the Newark store was open during the evenings so that the buyers could do their Christmas shopping."

Even the store's signature outdoor clock, located at the corner of Market and Halsey Streets, was not operational by the late 1970s. One of the store's most memorable latter-day figures was situated just inside the Bank Street revolving doors. A nun sat on a small chair and held a collection box. "It was always the same nun," remembers Allan. "She wore a traditional habit and did not actively solicit." If a donation to an orphanage was made, she would say a quiet "God bless you." The nun was stationed near the circular staircase that led to the Dinette on lower level one. The Dinette was the only food service left in the massive building. "Table service was eventually

Rose Della Virginia of Nutley worked a new Sensormatic anti-theft device at the downtown Newark Bamberger's in 1981. By the early 1980s, customer and employee pilferage heavily impacted sales figures at the downtown store. *Courtesy of the Newark Public Library.*

Penny Cruz of Newark stands next to an anti-shoplifting station at the Washington Street entrance. The May 1981 image shows the first-floor food department in the background. *Courtesy of the Newark Public Library.*

added because buyers had no place to entertain clients," says Allan. In 1979, Bamberger's fading Newark flagship developed plans for a renovated street floor. The company wanted to install new carpeting and clean the marble, but the modest renovation was tabled when a fire on June 14, 1979, at the Macy's Herald Square store caused over $5 million in damage and merchandise loss. The challenging situation at Hahne's Broad Street flagship was similar to Bamberger's on Market Street. Newark's oldest department store stood "a bit shopworn, mixed among the wig and record shops and shoeshine stands on Broad Street." The store also served as its corporate headquarters and did a respectable business during the lunchtime hours. But according to advertising director Robert Austin, "The old showcases and décor [at the Newark store] show that Hahne's invests more of its dollars in the suburban stores."[117] By 1980, the once sedate and staid department store had expanded its appeal to younger and more fashion-forward customers and was rewarded with sales figures that outpaced inflation.

As the 1970s came to a close, Bamberger's continued its expansion into the Philadelphia market. A 220,000-square-foot store opened as an anchor at the Montgomery Mall, located between Philadelphia and Allentown, on August 10, 1978. A 216,000-square-foot location at the Christiana Mall, outside Wilmington, Delaware, followed. The department store labeled its expansion into new and developing markets as "assertive" and touted its success as a store that "appealed chiefly to the middle to upper income shopper."[118] It offered a "store within a store concept" that featured "different shops at different stores depending on local enthusiasm." In the Philadelphia market, Bamberger's challenged longtime area retailers John

Wanamaker and Strawbridge & Clothier for department store industry dominance. Bamberger's Philadelphia market stores usually bested the rivals in the same shopping malls and in some cases outperformed the competition by almost 50 percent. At the Oxford Valley Mall in Langhorne, Pennsylvania, Bamberger's sales figures were often more than three times that of the neighboring Gimbels store. One unidentified Philadelphia department store executive told the *Philadelphia Bulletin*, "Bamberger's has taken a strong foothold in the Philadelphia retailing market at the expense of the older traditional retailers....Bamberger's [has emerged] as a retail force to be contended with in the Philadelphia market."[119] Drexel University professor Mercia Grassi recalls, "[Bamberger's] was a breath of fresh air in Philadelphia. They knew what they were doing at a time when many [Philadelphia department stores] didn't know what they were doing."

In 1980, Bamberger's success as a major fashion retailer that offered large inventories came at the expense of its older unit at the Princeton Shopping Center. The closing of the Princeton store was no surprise to the community and retail experts. The Princeton Bamberger's, built in 1954, was a two-level store that was only one-quarter the size of the nearby Quaker Bridge Mall location. "[Regardless of its small size,] Princeton needed more TLC

Shoppers gathered at the mall entrance of the new Christiana Mall store in Delaware on August 10, 1978. The new location displayed Bamberger's modern signage and was the most southern branch at the time of its opening. *Collection of the author.*

in order to do any business and give it a little sizzle," says Handler. The Princeton store closed in May 1980, and its lease was transferred to M. Epstein of Morristown, New Jersey. Epstein's proved to be a good fit in the fifty-five-store Princeton Shopping Center. Epstein's small size suggested "warmth and intimacy."[120]

Bamberger's entered the 1980s as a prosperous and progressive retailer, with a few exceptions. Its large Newark store showed no sign of a retail rebirth, and its older Morristown and Plainfield units were only half the size of a standard Bamberger store. But the R.H. Macy organization had a wonderful decade. The New York division reversed years of stagnation. Bamberger's continued its dominance in New Jersey and aggressively entered new markets. The San Francisco headquarters enjoyed the legacy left by former division president Ed Finkelstein. Additionally, Davison's was a formidable competitor to Rich's in Atlanta, and the Lasalle's and Kansas City stores posted modest profits. With annual sales gains over 12 percent, R.H. Macy & Co. became a corporation focused on the fashion merchandising of apparel and home furnishings with a reduced emphasis on budget and lower-margin lines of merchandise. The 1960s management team at Bamberger's was able to re-form the parent corporation and turn the middle-of-the-road department store organization into a profitable and reborn retail powerhouse.

Chapter 10

More Than Just a Place to Work

Successful department stores fostered family relationships, whether it was between customers, employees or both. Many former employees at Bam's fondly recall events and programs that the department store offered or sponsored. An employee handbook from the early 1980s detailed the benefits of being part of the Bamberger retail family:

> *Retailing is an exciting business, and Bamberger's is one of the most vigorous and progressive companies in the industry. Founded in 1892, we've blossomed into one of the largest and fastest growing department stores in the country. We owe this spectacular growth to our employees, who have succeeded in earning the loyalty and confidence of three generations of Bamberger's customers. Our recognition of this contribution is reflected in our modern, equitable personnel practices and employee benefits. We have rules, of course, to maintain the high standards of service and efficient operation that have made us a great department store, but you will see that all the regulations are just good common sense and are easy to follow.*

Bamberger's offered many special perks and activities for its employees, in addition to health and wealth benefit participation for those who were eligible. The Employee Activities Committee helped plan trips, luncheons and parties; store ambassadors were workers who earned special recognition for service and sales; a Better Job Bureau helped management identify employees with ambitions for job promotion; Rotating Employee Discussion

Groups provided feedback opportunities for change and improvement at the store level; and a Twenty-five-Year Club celebrated longtime and loyal employees with awards and a banquet. Store executives on the sales floor wore white flowers and helped serve customers and employees with particular questions or needs. The employee handbook informed new members of its workforce:

> *It might be helpful for you to remember that since 1892, thousands and thousands of men and women have worked for Bamberger's, and if most of them hadn't been successful in their jobs, Bamberger's itself couldn't have become the success it has. Bamberger's is a growing organization. We want you to grow with us. Both your future and Bamberger's are in your hands....You'll meet a lot of new people at Bamberger's and develop some new friendships. Bamberger's is more than "just a place to work."*

Bamberger's forged ahead in the 1980s with new locations that included a new trading area. In 1963, the King of Prussia Plaza opened near Valley

Bamberger's Cherry Hill had an unusual mall entrance during its first two decades of operation. Since the Bamberger name was unfamiliar to many South Jersey customers, the store opted to simply spell out its name and not use its famous signature font. This image from 1979 shows the interior mall entrance before a massive remodeling. *Photograph by the author.*

120

Forge, in Philadelphia's western suburbs. The outdoor plaza housed the nation's first full-line JCPenney department store and, over time, was joined by E.J. Korvette, Gimbels and John Wanamaker department stores. As the King of Prussia Plaza grew in size throughout the 1970s, it required a major renovation to remain competitive in the Philadelphia market. Mall developers designed an upscale Court at King of Prussia located next door to the existing plaza. The two centers were intended to complement each other. The new Court at King of Prussia featured Bamberger's and New York–based department stores Bloomingdale's and Abraham and Straus as its original anchors. On March 12, 1981, Bamberger's made its King of Prussia debut. The grand opening featured celebrities Chita Rivera, Ron Jaworski, Peter Duchin and Reggie Leach. When the Court at King of Prussia officially opened in August 1981, Carol Channing cut a diamond-studded ribbon and descended a staircase to the tune of "Hello Dolly," while designers Calvin Klein, Bill Blass and Oscar de la Renta arrived by helicopter. Mall officials dubbed it "the downtown of the suburbs" and expected the court to "restructure shopping patterns in the Pennsylvania suburbs."[121] The two adjoining centers offered 2.4 million square feet of retail space at a construction and renovation cost of $150 million. Bamberger's King of Prussia became a "great store" for the company and was one of the department store's highest-grossing locations.

Bamberger's entered the Baltimore market in 1981. Baltimore was home to several local department stores, including Hutzler's, Hecht's, Hochschild's and Stewart's, but Bamberger officials saw opportunities in a few planned shopping centers in the city's northern suburbs. The company felt that "metropolitan Baltimore can absorb additional retailers of its type despite the heavy competition."[122] On August 12, 1981, Bamberger's opened its first Maryland location at White Marsh, the first enclosed mall with five anchor department stores in the Baltimore area. Besides the new Bamberger's, White Marsh featured 190 stores and restaurants, along with anchors Sears, JCPenney, Washington-based Woodward & Lothrop and the matriarch of Baltimore department stores, Hutzler's. On opening day, shoppers flooded Bamberger's, promoted as a "full department store with traditional, trend-setting, and innovative merchandise," instead of the new Hutzler's store.[123] It was the beginning of the end for locally owned Hutzler's. When Bamberger's first studied the Baltimore market, the company recognized that its strongest competition was Hutzler's longtime suburban store in Towson.[124] Hutzler's Towson was the highest-grossing department store in the Baltimore area, and its annual sales figures rivaled some of Bamberger's best branches in the Philadelphia area. But Hutzler's Towson store was in need of renovation, and the family-owned business did not have the resources that Bamberger's enjoyed as a division of R.H. Macy & Co. The White Marsh Bamberger's store was quickly followed by another Baltimore location at the Hunt Valley Mall. Located approximately twenty miles north of downtown Baltimore, the 201,000-square-foot store opened on September 17, 1981. Peter Nero and members of the Baltimore Colts football team were on hand for the store's grand opening. When Bamberger's opened its two Baltimore locations in 1981, it sought talent from other established retailers. Five former Hutzler's buyers were recruited for the White Marsh store, and some former Stewart's buyers joined the team at Hunt Valley. Stewart's, owned by Associated Dry Goods, the parent of Hahne's, had been in a retrenchment mode, and the loss of these staff members was a blow to the organization. "At that point, the writing was on the wall for Stewart's," according to one former Bamberger's Hunt Valley employee. By November 1982, Associated Dry Goods had announced that its Stewart's division was ceasing operations, and its remaining stores were converted to the Caldor discount store format. Bamberger's counted on the same sales success in Baltimore that it enjoyed in Philadelphia, despite the area's established competition. Though Bamberger's White Marsh posted impressive sales figures, the Hunt Valley store did not meet sales expectations. When the Hunt Valley Mall initially opened in September 1981, the center was only 50 percent occupied. After almost thirty years of successful suburban expansions, Bamberger's experienced its first true misstep at the Hunt Valley store. "We were on a roll and we saw an opportunity in Baltimore," recalls Handler. "But [especially at Hunt Valley,] the customers were not as quick to respond."

Back in Newark, the flagship Bamberger's maintained its split image as a successful corporate headquarters with a downsized department store space that offered the company's lower-priced merchandise. "If you wanted something from Ralph Lauren [in Newark], they'd send you to Livingston or Paramus," says Allan. In January 1983, the Downtown Club, located in the store's tenth-floor restaurant space, closed. The walnut-paneled Downtown Club had operated out of Bamberger's old dining room since 1955, but dwindling membership at the private club contributed to its demise. The exclusive club had a history of discriminatory practice regarding membership. "[When I was mayor,] I was invited to lunch at the Downtown Club but I refused to go," says former mayor Kenneth A. Gibson. Gibson, an African American, says that Bamberger's "made them move." Bamberger's

Crowds filled the lower level at the Newark store during a November 1984 clearance sale. By the 1980s, Bamberger's had transitioned its former basement store into an automatic markdown format similar to Filene's Basement in Boston. *Courtesy of the Newark Public Library.*

decided that the former restaurant space would be best utilized as an in-house executive dining room.

The downtown Newark shopping district was dealt another blow in November 1981 when Two Guys announced its closure. Located on Broad Street in the former Kresge building, the Newark closing was part of a company decision that shuttered eighteen locations. Two Guys, a New Jersey and East Coast landmark discount store chain owned by Vornado, Inc., suffered from increased competition, aging suburban stores and an uninterested owner. As early as 1976, Two Guys had closed one of its sales floors and reduced its evening closure to 7:00 p.m. at the Newark store. The public-private group Renaissance Newark, Inc. complained that the twelve-story Kresge building, which also housed state and private offices on its upper floors, "is a major building in downtown Newark which over the years has continued to deteriorate." Renaissance Newark chairman Robert Van Fossan called the Kresge building "a major eye-sore in the city."[125] Customers and sales staff condemned the store's closure. "It's hard to believe," stated one sales clerk. "There aren't enough places in Newark for poor people to shop or to get discounts."[126] The Newark Two Guys ceased operations, along with the rest of the company's stores, on February 8, 1982.

Buyer Ken Allan left Bamberger's and joined the staff at Hahne's from 1982 until 1984. In 1983, he and a group of Hahne's staff members took a walk to Bamberger's to inspect the condition of the Newark store. The Hahne's buyers found that radical changes had occurred at Bamberger's. "The store had abolished better merchandise. The lower level and fourth floor had become 'corporate clearance.' Regularly priced merchandise was only located from the first to third floors." One of Allan's tasks at Hahne's included a visit to Hudson's flagship store in downtown Detroit. J.L. Hudson Co. was the world's second-largest department store, and the city had suffered many of the same social and economic challenges that faced Newark. After decades of retrenchment and diminishing sales, Hudson's closed its downtown Detroit landmark in January 1983. Allan was charged by Hahne's to learn how to close a large store. "Hahne's [Newark flagship store] always wanted to present a proper image with windows and American flags," recalls Allan. "But when you went inside the store, parts of the carpet were ready to disintegrate." By the mid-1980s, Bamberger's and Hahne's were not eager to abandon their Newark flagships. Hahne's owned its building, and Bamberger's had a "ridiculously cheap" long-term lease. Newark's proximity to New York City also served as a benefit to the two department stores. "Bamberger's and Hahne's kept their stores because the buyers were located so close to New York. They figured that they also might as well just run the store," says Allan.

During the early 1980s, R.H. Macy & Co. initiated a consolidation period that involved some of its weaker performing divisions. In May 1981, Macy's combined the operating headquarters of its Lasalle & Koch stores in Toledo with its Macy's Kansas City division. Lasalle's had been part of the R.H. Macy & Co. organization since 1924 and was its first expansion outside New York City. In addition to the loss of Lasalle's local buying and management team, all Toledo-area stores were converted to the Macy's nameplate. The newly combined Toledo and Kansas City division was renamed Macy's Midwest. "We all knew each other from the different divisions, but the properties in Kansas City and Toledo were hardly equal to ours," says former president Handler. The large downtown Toledo former flagship store was reduced from eleven floors to four selling floors. Customers complained that, since the merger, "the store hadn't been merchandised well" and "the inventory had been so slim that it became hard to buy anything."[127] After years of rumors and denials, Macy's closed the downtown Toledo store on January 28, 1984. In July 1985, Macy's sold the remaining Lasalle's to Dayton's Elder-Beerman stores. One market analyst stated, "[Macy's is] geared up to grow elsewhere and made a determination they were never going to be a factor in Ohio."[128] Macy's

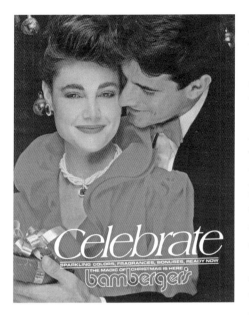

By the 1980s, Bamberger's, under the urging of its corporate parent Macy's, was issuing specific holiday and merchandise supplements. This *The Magic of Christmas Is Here* circular dates from the 1984 holiday season. *Courtesy of the Newark Public Library.*

Kansas City stores fared no better than the Toledo stores. The Kansas City division showed stagnant sales growth and contributed little to corporate profits. In February 1985, the company's Davison's Atlanta stores assumed control of the Kansas City division. Davison's was a strong performer for the R.H. Macy organization and was dubbed "aggressive." One retail analyst stated, "Hopefully some of the skills in Atlanta will rub off [in Kansas City]." Macy's Kansas City stores were often described as "run-of-the-mill" and "[visually] ten years behind the times."[129] The loss of the management team to Atlanta appeared to be a last-ditch effort to keep Macy's thirty-eight-year relationship with Kansas City viable. Four hundred Kansas City–based executives lost their jobs in the merger. The consolidation with the Atlanta stores yielded minimal improvement, and Macy's twelve Kansas City stores were sold to Dillard's in early 1986. The loss of the longtime Toledo and Kansas City stores gave Macy's a chance to focus on other opportunities. The R.H. Macy Corporation felt that its future was in new markets such as Miami, Dallas and Houston.

The early success at Bamberger's and Macy's was based on large inventories of popular goods, a large local buyer team at each store and vivid store display presentations. Officials acknowledged that this level of investment carried some financial risk. When fears of renewed inflation and increased interest rates created sluggish 1984 holiday sales, Macy's divisions throughout the country suffered. Macy's relied on heavy price cutting in order to move stalled merchandise. In 1985, overall company profits dropped by approximately 55 percent.[130] In some ways, Macy's, Bamberger's and Davison's stores were no longer unique. Competitors imitated their success, and Macy's was forced to consider further consolidations in order to protect the company and its investments.

Chapter II

The Last Bastion of Market Street

The year 1985 proved to be a pivotal one for the R.H. Macy & Co. organization. Even though the company had disposed of its longtime Toledo and Kansas City operations, many changes and events occurred behind the scenes. In spite of weak 1984 holiday season sales figures in the retail industry, Macy's held firm with its previously successful formula of carrying large inventories of fashion-oriented merchandise. R.H. Macy chairman Edward Finkelstein, the former vice-president of merchandise and sales promotion at Bamberger's and former "turn-around" president of Macy's San Francisco, assured stockholders that the corporation was not worried about the setbacks. "Risks are always there [in retailing]," stated Finkelstein.[131] However, Finkelstein was working on a plan that would permanently change the structure at R.H. Macy & Co. On October 21, 1985, Finkelstein and other Macy executives announced a proposed $3.7 billion leveraged buyout by company management. Isadore Barmash, the legendary retail columnist at the *New York Times*, called the buyout plan "the most dramatic entrepreneurial play in retailing in some time."[132] The plan made R.H. Macy & Co. a wholly independent company with debt obligations of $300 to $400 million annually. In order to honor the high debt payments, the company assets were vulnerable to a possible sell-off. With a softening of the retail sector, analysts questioned the buyout. Finkelstein, the engineer of the acquisition, stated that the management's purchase would entice top executive talent to stay within the organization. However, during the consolidation of Macy's Kansas City stores into Atlanta's Davison's division, 23 executives were displaced as a cost-cutting measure. After struggling to find financing, the management's buyout was completed in July 1986. A total of 345 executives invested in the newly private department store organization, and Macy leaders looked to "cut costs wherever possible and look for potential savings." The cuts initially affected the advertising and accounting departments, and the company even considered abandoning its famous Thanksgiving Day Parade.[133]

In late 1985, R.H. Macy & Co. announced that Atlanta's Davison's stores would carry the Macy's nameplate. Davison's had been under Macy's corporate ownership since 1925 but, like Toledo's former Lasalle & Koch stores, operated under its original name. Davison's always faced stiff competition from Atlanta's iconic Rich's, and the Davison's name helped distance itself from its New York ownership. Davison's president Leslie Ball told reporters, "I don't think shoppers will be disappointed by the name change. They'll think well maybe Atlanta's grown up enough to have a Macy's."[134] Ball insisted that the name change was necessary as the company planned expansions throughout the southern states. Though Davison's was an Atlanta institution, the company now banked on the familiarity of Macy's. Ball stated, "We never would have changed the Davison's name if we had not moved into the New Orleans and Alabama markets." Former Macy's executive Mark S. Handler says, "In Atlanta, we were the small guy [as compared to Rich's]. It was a pretty store downtown, but changing the name to Macy's was the right thing to do." By the end of 1985, R.H. Macy's operated four divisions: Macy's New York, Macy's San Francisco, Macy's Atlanta and Bamberger's, the only one of the four groups that held onto its original and popular name.

The department store industry experienced many changes during the mid-1980s that included multiple mergers and closures of well-established storied retailers. Canadian real estate developer Robert Campeau, in another highly leveraged and risky buyout, purchased Allied Stores Corporation, the parent of Stern's, Jordan Marsh, Maas Brothers and over twenty other smaller divisions across the country. Campeau immediately sold off most of the Allied divisions in order to finance the purchase. Ohrbach's was sold by its Dutch owner, Brenninkmeyer, and B. Altman & Co. and Bonwit Teller were purchased and eventually liquidated by the Australian real estate organization L.J. Hooker. May Department Stores acquired Associated Dry Goods, the corporate owner of Hahne's, Lord & Taylor, Robinson's and many other divisions, and British American Tobacco liquidated Gimbels, Macy's once-powerful rival.

Gimbels operated in the New York, Philadelphia, Pittsburgh and Milwaukee markets and competed head to head with Bamberger's at its only northern New Jersey store, located at Paramus's Garden State Plaza. Retail analysts predicted Gimbels' demise as the company lost considerable market share and executive talent. Gimbels' middle-class clientele abandoned the department store in favor of improved discount store retailers or higher-end, aggressive stores like Bamberger's and Lord & Taylor. Former Bamberger's president Rudolph Borneo recalls one visit to Gimbels in 1985: "I remember going into Gimbels [at Garden State Plaza] and saw how the clearance racks had been moved closer to the aisles, and I felt that Gimbels had moved closer to going out of business." Gimbels began its liquidation in June 1986, and the anticipated vacancy offered an opportunity for Associated Dry Goods to relocate its Hahne's flagship store and corporate offices to the soon-to-be-vacated Gimbels in Garden State Plaza. Hahne's was the area's only large department store retailer that didn't operate in Bergen County. Hahne's "agonized" over its planned departure from downtown Newark, but the retail portion of the building was "losing too much money."[135] It was the only one of Hahne's eight locations that was unprofitable. "When Hahne's announced that they were closing Newark, they did so before they were supposed to," says Allan. Though Gimbels employees knew that the company's closure was inevitable, Hahne's announced the move to Paramus before they were notified. The proposed move from Newark to Paramus occurred at the same time May Department Stores acquired Hahne's parent, Associated Dry Goods. May initially hesitated to follow through with the relocation plan, but in quick fashion, two out of three levels of the former Gimbels location were renovated. Hahne's kept its Newark store open, operating on one floor only, until October 8, 1987, when Hahne's opened its new Paramus flagship store, amid "bagpipes, banjo players, a parade, and full racks of carefully arranged merchandise." Located in Bergen County, the city of Paramus still strictly followed the county's voter-mandated Sunday blue law restrictions. "They didn't realize that their [Hahne's] offices couldn't be open on Sundays," states Allan. Its corporate offices were forced to remain in the Newark store after the store's retail closure. Newark's once-thriving business district was left with one department store.

Bamberger's continued its expansion throughout the mid-Atlantic states. The department store announced two future New Jersey units: Bridgewater Commons and the new Hamilton Mall, located about twenty minutes west of Atlantic City. The planned large Bridgewater store was located only about twelve miles from the smaller 1954 Plainfield store. The company also agreed to build two additional Baltimore-area stores and enter the Washington market. As it expanded into the Baltimore/Washington corridor, some longtime area retailers criticized its expansion. After Alvin Miller, owner of Baltimore's Princess Shops, referred to Bamberger's as "foreigners" in a *Baltimore Sun* editorial, the company responded, "To refer to our organization as 'foreigners' to Maryland is perhaps the most serious and uninformed claim that has been brought to the attention of the Maryland citizenry.…The minute we decided to build our first store in Maryland in the White Marsh Mall, we in fact became good citizens of Maryland by creating jobs for Maryland citizens, additional income for families and new sources of tax revenue for the county."[136] Questions arose when R.H. Macy & Co. confirmed its entry into Washington. The company committed to three locations: Tysons II in Fairfax County, Pentagon City and Springfield, Virginia. However, the corporation announced that the Tysons II store would operate as a Macy's, while the other two locations would be Bamberger's stores. Analysts predicted that all new Washington stores would assume the Macy's name but doubted that the company would abandon the strong name recognition of Bamberger's for its stores north of Baltimore.[137] Bamberger's opened its newest store in the upscale Owings Mills Mall, north of Baltimore, on July 30, 1986. The company called its new Owings Mills store "a new standard in retailing, a store where selling is viewed as an art and customer service is a company commitment," and offered "three floors of fall fashion news, state-of-the-art electronics, the Market Place & more." Owings Mills was billed as "Bamberger's style, Baltimore's spirit, together in a great new store." The mall included a Saks Fifth Avenue store, but Baltimore's once-dominant department store Hutzler's was shut out of the project.

On August 15, 1986, Macy's officials announced that the Bamberger name would be replaced and the New Jersey division would be renamed Macy's New Jersey. Bamberger's chairman Robert N. Friedman stated, "Three generations of families in our trading area have come to Bamberger's since it became a part of Macy's. They know our commitment to quality, selection, and service. They should also know that none of that is changing."[138] Friedman stressed that the name change was necessary as the company continued its growth. "[Macy's] has wider, immediate recognition as we expand beyond our trading area. We are on the threshold of an exciting new era," said Friedman. Friedman claimed that the move into the Washington market influenced the decision. "It was that expansion into a new trade area [Washington] that prompted the name change. We're

Bamberger's opened its third Baltimore-area store in August 1986 at the Owings Mills Mall. Only two months later, the Bamberger's name was officially changed to Macy's. The store, along with the entire once-upscale mall, is currently empty. *Collection of the author.*

entering Washington with a universally known name. It's really a much better name than Bamberger's as we enter new markets." The change was not entirely unexpected. The company had been advertising jointly in numerous New York papers as Macy's/Bamberger's, and the switch from Davison's to Macy's in Atlanta made the change inevitable. Macy's stated that the name change would become official on October 5, as every former Bamberger's store would have at least one Macy's sign installed by that date. All Bamberger's signs would be removed by November 15, 1986. The news did not surprise former Bamberger's buyer Jeanette Thomas. "I left [Bamberger's] in 1984, but it had really already become Macy's. It was in transition, but the paperwork still said Bamberger's." Friedman insisted that the change was in name only. "We will never lose sight of our [New Jersey] roots, our Bamberger's heritage. We are very proud of the name we were born with," stated Friedman. One industry analyst referred to the name change as "a melancholy reminder of how tradition can be erased by executive decree. Sacrificing the Bamberger's name [is] like abandoning a favorite relative."[139] Friedman also wanted to end any

In October 1986, R.H. Macy & Co. put the corporate name on the Bamberger's stores and slowly consolidated functions with the New York division. This photograph shows the imposing headquarters store in Newark just one month before the transition to Macy's. *Photograph by the author.*

rumors that the company would pull its headquarters out of Newark. Friedman told reporters, "We will be there [Newark] forever, as far as I can tell. It's a great location. We made the decision several years ago for the long-term that we'd keep the headquarters there. So it will be a long, long time, or forever, whichever comes first."

In early October 1986, the company's newspaper advertisements stated, "Bamberger's is taking the family name." Borneo states that the name change from Bamberger's to Macy's was not a simple decision. He recalls, "[Macy's chairman] Ed [Finkelstein] called me into New York and asked me what I thought about changing Bamberger's into Macy's. I told him that it would help make Macy's a national brand and market. But Ed said that that wasn't the answer that he expected. But I told him emotionally I wasn't thrilled. The name change was hard on an emotional basis, especially for the customers and workers." Borneo recalls one visit to the Ocean County Mall store after the news broke. "I was in Ocean County, and a man saw that I was the store president. He told me that he couldn't believe that I let them change the name. Bamberger's was a much better company! I told him that Bamberger's had always been a part of Macy's, and he just looked at me. Most people didn't know that we were already a part of Macy's."

The Macy's New Jersey division continued its expansion with another Baltimore-area location. On February 25, 1987, the store opened at the

Shoppers wait outside the Market Street Bamberger's entrance in 1986. The intersection of Market and Halsey Streets was home to a popular New Jersey Transit downtown bus stop. *Photograph by the author.*

Above: Bamberger's signature font graces the exterior of the Cherry Hill Mall store. The 1962 Cherry Hill Bamberger's was its first and only Philadelphia/South Jersey location for many years. *Photograph by the author.*

Below: Bamberger's was officially renamed Macy's on October 5, 1986. At the August 1986 name change announcement, Macy's pledged that every former Bamberger's location would have at least one Macy's sign by the transition date. The Cherry Hill Mall store is shown in this photograph with the Macy's name on the south side and the Bamberger's logo on the east side. *Photograph by the author.*

Marley Station Mall in Glen Burnie. Grand opening festivities included appearances by Robin Leach and Miss America Kellye Cash, and grand opening advertisements read, "Macy's style, Maryland's spirit." The three Washington-area stores had planned openings for 1988, and stores in Freehold and Bridgewater, New Jersey, awaited completion. Executives who invested in the management buyout eagerly awaited the financial rewards and worked hard to increase sales and profits that could make interest payments on the debt. The company made adjustments to its image and offerings, reduced inventories of fashion-conscious merchandise and actively pursued promotional discounts as a means to cut costs.[140] One cost-cutting measure came at the expense of Macy's New Jersey division. The company announced a merger of the New York and New Jersey divisions in April 1988. The divisional merger was in strong contrast to former Bamberger's chairman Robert Friedman's 1986 announcement that Newark would always remain a headquarters operation. R.H. Macy & Co. chairman Finkelstein reported, "There will be a substantial number of people [in Newark and New York] who will be surplus, but we hope to relocate many of them in other divisions."[141] The consolidation eliminated approximately one hundred buyers, merchandise managers and other executives. The savings from the merger were intended to fund Macy's $1.1 billion acquisition of Los Angeles's Bullock's and Bullock's Wilshire/I. Magnin stores. However, the merger of the New York and New Jersey divisions was best described as "chaotic." Macy's New Jersey stores utilized IBM registers that precisely tracked inventory and sales histories. Macy's New York used NCR machines. The IBM and NCR computers were incompatible, and the two divisions were unable to share sales and inventory information. In addition, the Bullock's purchase from debt-ridden Federated Department Stores and its new owner, Robert Campeau, only added to Macy's debt and performance pressure.

Unable to satisfy creditors, increase sales and make highly leveraged debt payments, R.H. Macy & Co. filed for Chapter 11 bankruptcy protection on January 27, 1992. The company promised business as usual at its approximately 250 department, specialty and boutique stores, but the $3.6 billion debt load implied future organizational and managerial changes. The bankruptcy filing allowed the corporation to pay operating bills and employee salaries, break store lease obligations and resume merchandise shipments, especially from those manufacturers that had stopped deliveries due to delinquent bills.[142] Fearing that he would be forced out of the company, Edward Finkelstein left the organization three months after the bankruptcy

By the mid-1970s, Bamberger's had bricked over most of its display windows around the exterior of the Newark store. Repeated acts of vandalism and theft left the building looking like a sealed-off fortress. This photograph shows the Newark location, renamed Macy's, before its 1992 closure. *Courtesy of the Newark Public Library.*

filing. The Macy's board had lost faith in its leader, and he became an "easy target" for corporate backlash.[143] Finkelstein had spent his entire career at R.H. Macy, and the company's many peaks and valleys defined his tenure. His departure was swift and surprised industry analysts.

Viewed as a "black hole into which money disappeared," the Newark operation appeared vulnerable to closure.[144] Although the building no longer housed a divisional headquarters, and in spite of its struggling and diminishing retail component, a $7 million corporate data processing facility was completed on its upper floors. The data processing investment gave Newark leaders and employees hope that the Newark operation would not become a bankruptcy casualty. Store management in Newark, Morristown and Plainfield, the three oldest former Bamberger's stores, worried about the future. All were either antiquated, obsolete or both. After Macy's announced in early May 1992 that 10 of its 120 department stores would likely close, Newark leaders appealed to corporate management, contending that the Newark operation was essential to the city's economic health. City officials and community groups in Morristown and Plainfield also mobilized to prevent any closure decisions in their communities. A Macy's Appreciation Campaign that publicly celebrated the company's "long-term civic involvement in the city" was quickly organized in Newark.[145] On May 18, 1992, volunteers from Renaissance Newark gathered outside the Newark store and collected signatures from 275 shoppers, residents and office workers who eagerly signed the petition in support of the downtown store and promising a future commitment to the retail store. Newark mayor Sharpe James stated, "We want Macy's [corporate] management to understand that this store is an integral part of downtown life and also an important source of jobs. We see this as a crucial appeal to Macy's to carefully consider Newark's renaissance of the last five years and the city-inspired recent relocation of 2,500 state employees within a short walking distance of its Newark store as they weigh this restructuring."[146] Two days later, R.H. Macy & Co. announced that the Newark store, along with its longtime Plainfield location, would close by July 30, 1992.

Employees and customers in Newark expressed dismay but little surprise at the decision. After almost one hundred years of operation, the former Bamberger store had transitioned "from a jewel of the carriage trade to a last

A rare photograph shows the main floor of the Newark store shortly before its 1992 closing. The main floor had received little remodeling since a 1966 rearrangement of departments. By 1992, the massive Newark former flagship store had been reduced to only four selling floors. *Photograph by the author.*

By 1992, the once-massive housewares department at the Newark store had been relocated to a small section on the third floor. *Photograph by the author.*

resort for slow-selling items." The downtown Newark location predominantly catered to office workers during their lunch breaks and city residents who had limited shopping options and relied on public transportation. A *New York Times* article best described the store upon the closing announcement. "At the end yesterday, a floorwalker could roll a bowling ball down almost any aisle at Macy's in Newark and not hit anyone," reported Charles Strum. "The Cellar, Macy's famous Manhattan basement of exotic food and state-of-the-art pots and pans, was reduced to a small section of china, glassware, and small appliances on the second floor here. The real basement in Newark was closed to shoppers, as were 12 of the 16 floors in the block-square building on Market Street....With the closing, Newark has lost the last and perhaps most potent symbol of a once-glorious mercantile history and suffered another blow in its attempt to restore an economy that fled with its middle class two decades ago."[147] Mayor James met with Macy's corporate management in New York and tried to reverse the decision but was unsuccessful. Macy's pledged to keep its data processing and payroll centers open in the building, but the retail portion would permanently close. "By 1992, everybody knew that the Newark store had no long-term value," says Borneo. "Newark was a great store. It had many great years and had a great run." The final day at the former downtown Bamberger's store was August 7, 1992. The store closed one day early because "we simply ran out of merchandise." Approximately 340 Newark store employees retired, were transferred to other stores, or lost their jobs. It was the end of an era that began with Louis Bamberger in 1892.

In Plainfield, a group of residents organized the Keep Macy's in Plainfield Committee. The 1954 downtown Plainfield store employed approximately 150 workers and was the city's fourth-largest employer.[148] The former Bamberger's location was one of the last retail holdouts in a once vibrant downtown shopping district. Rosemary Friedrich recalls getting thirteen thousand signatures opposing the store closure in just a few days. "I sat outside the [Plainfield] store, handed out postcards and put on the stamps," she recalls. "Bamberger's had to hire a public relations firm just to deal with us! We felt that it was so important to keep that store. Employees were grateful that we were trying to do something for the store. [Macy's] didn't seem to care about us, but they were a little embarrassed." Corporate management insisted the store had been unprofitable for the

In 1986, the New Jersey stores were officially named Macy's, and the once-iconic Newark store slowly lost its headquarters status. This image shows the Newark store in 1992 with the Macy's nameplate on the Market Street side of the building, looking toward Four Corners. *Photograph by the author.*

past few years, but the Keep Macy's in Plainfield Committee received conflicting information. "[One internal Macy's document acquired by the committee claimed] Plainfield was the highest-generating store [in terms of sales] by square foot," states Nancy Piwowar, head of the Historical Society of Plainfield. Although public documents did show that sales figures were down in Plainfield, the figures were much lower at most stores throughout the division. For example, while sales were down 2 percent in Plainfield, they were down 9 percent in Livingston. Despite the protests, Macy's refused to reverse its decision in Plainfield, and the business closed on August 1. Macy's hoped that Plainfield shoppers would transfer their business to the nearby Bridgewater and Menlo Park locations. Although Friedrich loved the Plainfield store, she states, "I haven't shopped at a Macy's since." Longtime customer Jeanne Locke bemoaned the closing of Plainfield's Bamberger's. Locke was also a frequent customer at Tepper's, which closed in the spring of 1977. "Bamberger's became my replacement store for Tepper's," says Locke. "Shopping [in Plainfield] was a pleasant experience. It was one-stop shopping for us. Stores today lack the character that these department stores had. I used to find just about anything in downtown Plainfield."

The former Bamberger's store at the Hunt Valley Mall in Maryland was another store on the 1992 closing list. The mall was a chronically troubled shopping center with high vacancy rates. Opened in 1981, the Hunt Valley store never met sales expectations, and management claimed that the 1986 Owings Mills store siphoned off its business. The store's summer 1992 closure ended an eleven-year run at Hunt Valley that paled in comparison to the company's presence in downtown Newark.

After the 1992 round of closings was released to the public, Morristown city and store officials breathed a sigh of relief that the 1949 landmark store on the Morristown Green would remain open. It was the smallest store in the former Macy's New Jersey division, and it suffered from persistent parking issues and nearby competition. The Morristown store's reprieve was brief. On March 2, 1993, Macy's announced that the Morristown store would close at the end of June and leave 170 workers unemployed. The closing in Morristown was, in some ways, the last piece of L. Bamberger & Co.'s legacy. When it opened in 1949, Bamberger's Morristown offered everything from "baby booties to a television set." With expansive merchandise offerings and services, the Morristown location had been an important piece of Bamberger's success and had helped the company add the additional byline "One of America's Great Stores."

As the R.H. Macy & Co. organization struggled through its bankruptcy reorganization and fought to remain independent, the corporation received an unsolicited offer from Federated Department Stores. Macy's wanted to acquire Federated back in 1988, but six years later, the tables were turned. A Federated/Macy's merger offered the new company greater purchasing power and a way to eliminate redundant managerial and buying positions. Federated continually acquired Macy's stock and built support for seven months until Macy's finally succumbed. The July 1994 merger resulted in a $14 billion corporation with 340 stores. Federated and Macy's had rarely overlapped geographic locations, and the combined company forces now dominated the Florida, California, mid-Atlantic and Northeast markets.

As part of the merger, Federated operated Macy's, Stern's, Bloomingdale's and Abraham and Straus stores in the New York/North Jersey market. In 1995, Federated merged Brooklyn's Abraham and Straus store into the Macy's nameplate, and in 2001, it converted Stern's to Macy's. As former

In 1996, the closed Newark store became 165 Halsey Street, one of the premier telecommunications centers in the country. The building's sturdy construction adequately supported large mechanical features that were necessary to operate the telecom/data center operation. Many ornate features on the building's exterior showed noticeable wear, and the once-signature clock had long since been removed. *Photograph by the author.*

The first floor of the Bamberger's building remains active along the Market Street side. A Rite Aid pharmacy, at the Market and Washington Street corner, has operated for many years, and urban wear stores fill out the rest of the lower floor. This picture was taken in December 2015. *Photograph by the author.*

Abraham and Straus and Stern's were folded into Macy's stores, Paramus became home to three Macy's stores in three separate enclosed malls, just four miles apart. The former Bamberger's store at the "puffed-up behemoth" Garden State Plaza was just a stone's throw away from its fierce neighboring competitor, the former Stern's at Bergen Mall. However, both were now under the same management and same nameplate. When the Bergen Mall Stern's converted to Macy's in 2001, longtime local customers complained that "they would rather go naked than buy clothing anywhere else." The Bergen Mall Stern's was a "refuge from the madness [at] the other malls." It was seen as an "old-fashioned emporium that prided itself on solid merchandise, sagacious sales help and the kind of clientele that cherished continuity in this mall-eat-mall world."[149] In March 2005, Macy's closed the former Stern's store at the Bergen Mall. The company cited the saturation of Macy's in the Paramus market.

Except for the Newark, Morristown, Plainfield and Princeton locations, all former Bamberger's stores currently operate as Macy's. Many shopping centers that housed earlier Bamberger's stores, such as Garden State Plaza, Menlo Park Mall and Cherry Hill, have been expanded and rebuilt beyond recognition. Since its acquisition by Federated Department Stores, Macy's has become a national brand. Critics complain that today's Macy's stores have "lost their identity" and "the glitter [from the 1970s] has disappeared."[150] Individual locations champion uniformity and carry clothing lines that are no longer unique and exclusive. Macy's New Jersey stores enjoy broad consumer loyalty and consistently strong sales figures.

Many shoppers still affectionately recall the Bamberger's or Bam's names. For almost one hundred years, the store belonged to the Garden State, and it was a large part of New Jersey's economic and social identity. The "Bamberger's Spirit" motivated the employees and provided the foundation of "One of America's Great Stores." Always operating with a tradition of integrity, honesty and principled ethics, the "Bamberger's Creed" of 1964 summarizes the company's formula for success and prosperity: "Whatever you buy, at whatever the price, when you buy from Bamberger's you're buying from New Jersey's greatest store, honor-bound to keep faith in every way with its customers."

Soup and Sandwich

Most Bamberger's stores contained popular dining facilities. Many suburban locations contained a Carriage House restaurant, later renamed Louis B's. The downtown Newark store lost its formal dining room in 1955 but served customers at fountain snack bars on the street level and fourth floors. A popular lunch counter named the Dinette was found on the store's lower level. As dining options decreased in downtown Newark, a table service room was added next to the Dinette, and the facility changed names to the Garden State Tea Room.

Bamberger's served relatively simple, good basic food at its restaurants. Hot dogs and orange drink in paper cones were popular at its snack bars. Many of the store's sandwiches were served on Pechter's bread. The following recipes are courtesy of one of the store chefs and were recalled by memory, not from food service recipe cards.

༄

CREAMY TOMATO BISQUE

2 medium to large tomatoes
46-ounce can Campbell's tomato juice
2 cups evaporated milk
margarine and flour
salt and pepper to taste

Boil tomatoes in a heavy pot in 1 cup of water. Cook until skin and seeds are easily removable. Discard remaining water. Add tomato juice and evaporated milk to cooked tomatoes and heat. Set aside a small amount of equal parts melted margarine and flour. Cook, but do not burn, margarine and flour in a separate skillet. Slowly add margarine/flour to tomato mixture until desired thickness is achieved. Add salt and pepper to taste.

CLAM BISQUE

Makes 4–5 servings

3 cups cream
1½ sticks margarine
1½ cups evaporated milk
1½ 10-ounce cans clam juice
onions, celery and tomatoes (modest amounts chopped to satisfaction)
3 (8-ounce) cans minced clams
salt and pepper to taste

Heat cream, margarine and evaporated milk in a double boiler. Add clam juice, onions and celery. Cook for at least 30 minutes. Add clams and tomatoes. Heat and season to taste.

SIMPLE STEAK SANDWICH

This sandwich was the most frequently ordered sandwich in the store's dining facilities.

½ medium yellow onion, chopped
½ pound very thinly sliced fresh or frozen beef
Kaiser roll
2 slices American or provolone cheese

Heat a small amount of oil in a skillet. Add onions and cook until soft. Add steak and cook for no more than two minutes. Place on a Kaiser roll. Add cheese to sandwich and place under grill until cheese is melted.

STUFFED MUSHROOMS, ITALIAN STYLE

This recipe was part of a "mushroom celebration" held during early 1970. "Mushrooms were fashion," and images were featured on pillows, tea towels, table accessories, alabaster paperweights and canisters, in addition to the jewelry and gift wrap departments. During this promotion, Bamberger's Carriage House restaurants added stuffed mushrooms to their menus.

1 pound (18 to 20) medium-sized fresh mushrooms
¼ cup lemon juice
1 cup soft bread crumbs
¾ cup canned Italian plum tomatoes, drained and chopped
½ cup chopped prosciutto
2½ tablespoons grated Parmesan cheese
1 tablespoon parsley flakes
½ teaspoon oregano flakes
¼ teaspoon ground black pepper
1 dash garlic powder
¼ cup olive oil

Rinse, pat dry and remove stems from mushrooms (reserve stems for use in soups, stews, etc.). Dip each cap in lemon juice. Combine remaining ingredients except oil; blend well. Fill each cap with about one heaping teaspoonful of bread crumb mixture. Arrange stuffed mushrooms in shallow baking dish or pie plate. Sprinkle with oil. Pour ¼ inch of hot water into the pan to prevent mushrooms from becoming dry. Bake in preheated hot oven (400 degrees Fahrenheit) for 15 minutes or until mushrooms are browned and heated throughout. Serve immediately.

Fried Chicken (Soul Food Night)

1 cup flour
½ teaspoon salt
¼ teaspoon pepper
2 teaspoons onion powder
2 teaspoons garlic powder
1 cup milk
1 egg
1 chicken, cut into pieces
vegetable oil

Combine flour, salt, pepper, onion and garlic powders. In a separate bowl, mix together milk and egg. Dunk chicken pieces in egg and roll in flour mixture. Fill a large cast-iron frying pan with vegetable oil, leaving two inches to the top of the pan. Heat oil to medium-high heat. Chicken should sizzle when added. Do not allow chicken to burn. Cook until chicken "bleeds out," turning once. Remove chicken when fully cooked and hang from wire for about 10 minutes.

Notes

Chapter 1

1. *Baltimore Sun*, "Louis Bamberger Succumbs at 88," March 12, 1944.
2. *Jewish Chronicle*, June 20, 1941.
3. Ibid.
4. Thomas Ankner, "Newark at 350: Settlement, Growth, Renewal," Newark Public Library website, 2016.
5. *Jewish Chronicle*, "Louis Bamberger's Contributions Inestimable," June 20, 1941.
6. Frank I. Liveright, "One of America's Great Stores," private document, circa 1940s, 2.
7. Ibid., 3.
8. William Starr Myers, *The Story of New Jersey* (New York: Lewis Historical Publishing Company, 1945), 557.
9. *Around the Clock*, "75 Years in the News," December 1967.
10. Liveright, "One of America's Great Stores," 6–8.
11. Ibid., 5.
12. *Jersey Journal*, advertisement, April 22, 1912.

Chapter 2

13. *Jersey Journal*, store advertisement, October 16, 1912.
14. Ibid., 12.

15. *New York Times*, "Rapid Growth in Newark's Business Centre Shown by Increase in Splendid Buildings," July 21, 1912.
16. *Jersey Journal*, "Bamberger's Fine New Store Formally Opened," October 16, 1912.
17. Ibid., advertisement, October 19, 1912.
18. John E. O'Connor and Charles F. Cummings, *Bamberger's Department Store, Charm Magazine, and the Culture of Consumption in New Jersey, 1924–1932* (Newark: New Jersey Historical Society, 1984), 4.
19. Newspaper advertisement, 1920.
20. *Trenton Times Advertiser*, "Three Residents of Trenton to Get Awards during WOR Tribute to City Tomorrow," January 26, 1947.
21. Liveright, "One of America's Great Stores," 16.
22. *Jewish Journal*, January 20, 1923.
23. *Charm*, February 1924.
24. Ibid., 1929.
25. Liveright, "One of America's Great Stores," 13.
26. *Jersey Journal*, advertisement, September 6, 1925.
27. Liveright, "One of America's Great Stores," 20.
28. R.H. Macy & Co. Annual Report, February 1, 1930.

Chapter 3

29. *Jersey Journal*, advertisement, October 16, 1913.
30. *Newark Evening News*, "L. Bamberger & Co. Reportedly Sold to R.H. Macy of New York," June 29, 1929.
31. *Newark Evening News*, "L. Bamberger & Co. Character will Be Perpetuated," July 1, 1929.
32. Ibid.
33. R.H. Macy & Co. Annual Report, January 1, 1925.
34. *Jewish Chronicle*, "Bamberger, Mrs. Fuld, Drop Institute Roles," March 30, 1934.
35. *New York Times*, "Rowland H. Macy, Merchant," March 31, 1877.
36. Ibid., "The Romance of a Great Business," August 20, 1922, BRM6.
37. Ibid., "Macy & Co. Buy Koster & Bial Site," July 17, 1901.
38. Ibid., "75 Years of Progress in the Life of a Great New Department Store," February 13, 1933.
39. *Jersey Journal*, "Santa Claus—He's Very Much in Evidence at Bamberger's," December 5, 1902.

40. *Newark Evening News*, "More than a Mile of Monsters Ready for Toy Parade," November 17, 1932.
41. John Cunningham, *Newark* (Newark: New Jersey Historical Society, 2002), 282.
42. *New York Times*, "Straus Optimistic on Retail Outlook," October 27, 1943, 31.

Chapter 4

43. Camilo José Vergara, *American Ruins* (New York: Monacelli Press, 1999), 28.
44. R.H. Macy & Co. Annual Report, 1944.
45. Ibid., 1945.
46. *San Francisco Chronicle*, "It's Macy's, S.F. Now," October 17, 1947, 19.
47. Miriam Pepper and Elaine Adams, "Macy's Closing Stirs Memories of Elegant Downtown Era," *Kansas City Star*, February 23, 1986.
48. Samuel Feinberg, *What Makes Shopping Centers Tick* (New York: Fairchild Publications, 1960), 120.
49. *Newark Evening News*, "New Bamberger Branch Opens in East Orange," April 16, 1945.
50. Ibid., "Bamberger's Opened," April 2, 1949.
51. Ibid., "Bamberger's Branch—Morristown, 1st Unit in Program of Expansion," September 2, 1947.
52. R.H. Macy & Co. Annual Report, 1950.
53. *Newark Evening News*, "New Bamberger Store," October 9, 1953.
54. Ibid., "Bam's Plainfield Store to Hold Open House," May 7, 1954.

Chapter 5

55. Robert Hetherington, "History of Hahne & Co.," *Newark Star-Ledger*, September 17, 1978.
56. Ibid.
57. *Jersey Journal*, Hahne & Co. advertisement, September 4, 1901.
58. *Jewish Chronicle*, "Hahne & Co. Ushers in 67th Big Year," October 9, 1925.
59. Ibid., "Hahne & Co. Will Undergo Many Great Changes," June 27, 1924.
60. *Jersey Journal*, Hahne & Co. advertisement, September 4, 1901.

61. Ted Hall, "Preview of Hahne Store," *Newark Evening News*, February 15, 1951.
62. *Jersey Journal*, L.S. Plaut advertisement, August 10, 1923.
63. *Trenton Times*, "S.S. Kresge Buys Big Newark Store," July 31, 1925.
64. Joan Cook, "Ohrbach's Will Close Store in Newark," *New York Times*, December 7, 1973.
65. *Newark Evening News*, "Hearns Opens New Store," September 2, 1937.
66. *New York Times*, "Altman Store Opened," March 31, 1931, 53.

Chapter 6

67. *New York Times*, "Noisy Crowd Halts Sale," February 16, 1946.
68. Donald Warshaw, "Newark's Lunch-Hour Mecca Shuts after 70 Years," *Newark Star-Ledger*, January 5, 1983.
69. Isadore Barmash, *Macy's for Sale* (New York: Weidenfeld & Nicholson, 1989), 46.
70. Feinberg, *What Makes Shopping Centers Tick*, 102.
71. Ibid.
72. Ibid., 99.
73. *Newark Evening News*, "Bamberger Branch in Paramus," December 22, 1954.
74. Feinberg, *What Makes Shopping Centers Tick*, 4.
75. *Newark Evening News*, "Bamberger's Will Close Millburn Store," September 26, 1957.
76. *New York Times*, "Bamberger's Officially Opens Menlo Park Store," September 9, 1959.
77. Barmash, *Macy's for Sale*, 47.
78. R.H. Macy & Co. Annual Report, 1965.
79. Ibid., 35.
80. *New York Times*, September 9, 1959.
81. Clarence Dean, "Evening Shopping Grows in Suburbs," *New York Times*, January 16, 1961, 29.
82. Alfred Lief, *Family Business* (New York: McGraw-Hill, 1968), 285.
83. Al Klimcke, "Bamberger Cherry Hill Opening Is a Cheery Event," *Newark Evening News*, September 21, 1962.
84. Barmash, *Macy's for Sale*, 58.
85. *Trenton Evening Times*, "New Fitch Way Center Gets Preliminary OK," December 31, 1963.

86. R.H. Macy & Co. Annual Report, 1965.

87. Vincent P. De Slavin, "Leisurely Shopping Gone but Stores Still Thrive," *Newark Evening News*, July 16, 1966.

88. Bill Whitworth, "Negro Manikin Newest Thing in Window Displays," *Toledo Blade*, August 17, 1964.

89. Cunningham, *Newark*, 312.

Chapter 7

90. Douglas Robinson, "King Warns Cities of Summer Riots," *New York Times*, April 17, 1967, 1.

91. *Trenton Times*, "Violence Continues in Newark," July 16, 1967.

92. John McLaughlin, "The Riot: Why and What Now?" *Trenton Times*, July 16, 1967.

93. Ibid.

94. Martin Gensberg, "Major Stores Closed in Newark as Few Decide to Go Downtown," *New York Times*, July 16, 1967.

95. Ibid.

96. David Rosenweig, "He Wonders: Can Lightning Strike Twice?" Associated Press, July 27, 1967.

97. Joe DiLeo, "Everybody Knows They Need Help," *Trenton Times*, April 2, 1973.

98. Ibid.

99. Ralph Blumenthal, "The Roar of Bulldozers Marks Rockland Growth," *New York Times*, March 25, 1969, 33.

Chapter 8

100. Thomas J. Hooper, "Business in Newark Hard Hit by Riots," *Newark Evening News*, July 16, 1967.

101. Gunter David, "Last Minute Bargain Hunters Abound as Chase Closes Up," *Newark Evening News*, February 12, 1968.

102. *Newark Evening News*, "Two Guys to Open Its Newark Store," September 3, 1968.

103. Barbara Kukla, "Bamberger's Livingston Store Opens with a Flourish," *Newark Star-Ledger*, October 5, 1971.

104. *New Jersey Information*, "Klein's Shuts Floors in Store," June 1973.

105. Joan Cook, "Ohrbach's Will Close Store in Newark, Cites Drop in Sales and Lack of Lease," *New York Times*, December 7, 1973.

106. Fred Ferrettis, "A New Mall, Maybe the Last, Rises for Shoppers," *New York Times*, December 10, 1972, 111.

107. Isadore Barmash, "Ohrbach's Opens Paramus Store," *New York Times*, August 18, 1967.

108. Norma Harrison, "$1 Million Roofed Mall Opens in Bergen," *New York Times*, September 16, 1973.

109. Ania Savage, "Garden State Plaza Will Enclose Mall," *New York Times*, February 23, 1975, NJ58.

110. Alfred E. Clark, "Sunday Business Target in New Jersey," *New York Times*, February 17, 1957.

Chapter 9

111. Barmash, *Macy's for Sale*, 62.

112. Lisa Hammel, "One Basement That's Looking Up," *New York Times*, November 15, 1976.

113. Isadore Barmash, "Macy's Catches Up to Lead the Parade," *New York Times*, July 24, 1977, F1.

114. *Trenton Times*, "Essex County Major Stores Vow Defiance Today," December 5, 1976.

115. *New York Times*, "Jersey Shoppers Out as Blue Laws End," November 12, 1979, B2.

116. Personal interview with Ken Allan.

117. David Allen, "Hahne's Rides Wave of Success with New Look," *Newark Star-Ledger*, September 28, 1980.

118. Warren Sloat, "Big Bang Theory of Bam's," *Trenton Times*, August 19, 1976.

119. Trudy Prokop, "Wanamaker Cites Competition, Opens on Holiday," *Philadelphia Bulletin*, May 25, 1975.

120. Jaye Scholl, "Bamberger's Will Shut in Princeton," *Trenton Times*, April 9, 1980.

Chapter 10

121. Ewart Rouse, "Elegant Mall Opens in Blaze of Promotions," *Philadelphia Inquirer*, August 2, 1981.

122. James Gutman, "Department Store Competition to Get Boost from 3 More Chains," *Baltimore Sun*, April 20, 1980.

123. *Baltimore Sun*, "Bamberger's Now in Baltimore," August 2, 1981.

124. Stacie Knable, "Hutzler's Wants to Have that Royal Feeling Again," *Evening Sun*, August 6, 1981.

125. *Newark Star-Ledger*, "Two Guys Homeless," April 20, 1981.

126. Frederick W. Byrd, "Two Guys Will Be Missed," *Newark Star-Ledger*, November 23, 1981.

127. *Toledo Blade*, "Lunchtime Shoppers to Decry Plan to Close Downtown Macy's Store," December 31, 1983.

128. Ben Marrtson, "4 Macy Stores in Area Sold to Dayton Firm," *Toledo Blade*, July 3, 1985.

129. Mike Hendricks, "Macy's Gearing Up for Comeback in Area," *Kansas City Star*, June 9, 1985.

130. Ibid.

Chapter 11

131. Barmash, *Macy's for Sale*, 92.

132. Isadore Barmash, "Macy's Buyout Still Up in Air," *New York Times*, November 11, 1985, D6.

133. Isadore Barmash, "A Leveraged Buyout Waits for the Parade," *New York Times*, January 25, 1987, F1.

134. Beverly Y. Hall, "Attention Shoppers: Davison's Is Macy's," *Atlanta Journal*, October 14, 1985.

135. Anne-Marie Cotlone, "Hahne's Bids a Farewell to Newark," *Newark Star-Ledger*, June 18, 1986.

136. *Baltimore Sun*, "Bamberger's & Maryland," March 10, 1983.

137. Caroline Mayer, "Macy's Is Moving into D.C. Area," *Washington Post*, February 9, 1985.

138. Scott Muldoon, "The New Macy's: Bamberger's Changes Name to Parent Firm," *Newark Star-Ledger*, September 4, 1986.

139. Jeffrey A. Trachtenberg, *The Rain on Macy's Parade* (New York: Random House, 1996), 137.

140. Barmash, "Leveraged Buyout Waits for the Parade," January 25, 1987.

141. *New York Times*, "Macy's Prepares for Takeover," April 26, 1988, D2.

142. Stephanie Storm, "Macy's Asks Court to Provide Shield Against Creditors," *New York Times*, January 28, 1992.

143. Trachtenberg, *Rain on Macy's Parade*, 224.

144. Ibid., 112.

145. Angela Stewart, "Renaissance Macy's Hopes to Keep Macy's Open," *Newark Star-Ledger*, May 19, 1992.

146. Ibid.

147. Charles Strum, "No Miracle on Market Street for Final Retail Holdout," *New York Times*, May 21, 1992.

148. Gabriel H. Gluck, "Plainfield Residents Campaign to Keep Macy's," *Newark Star-Ledger*, June 16, 1992

149. Andrew Jacobs, "Almost Like a Death in the Family," *New York Times*, February 11, 2001, 40.

150. Trachtenberg, *Rain on Macy's Parade*, 236.

Index

About the Author

Michael Lisicky is a nationally recognized department store historian, lecturer and author. His books have received critical acclaim in such major newspapers as the *Washington Post*, the *Philadelphia Inquirer*, the *Boston Globe*, the *Tampa Tribune* and the *Baltimore Sun*. His book *Gimbels Has It!* was cited as "one of the freshest reads of 2011" by National Public Radio's *Morning Edition* program. Lisicky has given lectures at such locations as the New York Public Library, the Boston Public Library, New York Fashion Week, the D.C. Public Library and the 2011 Wanamaker Organ Centennial Week celebration in Philadelphia. He also served as a historical consultant for the Oscar-nominated film *Carol* and has been featured in the *New York Times*, *Wall Street Journal*, on National Public Radio and on CBS's *Sunday Morning* television program. Lisicky resides in Baltimore, where he is also an oboist with the Baltimore Symphony Orchestra. He is the author of *Baltimore Symphony Orchestra: A Century of Sound*.

Visit us at
www.historypress.net
....

This title is also available as an e-book